Winston G Litchmore was born again in 1966 and has been involved in preaching, teaching the Scriptures, pastoral counselling and church administration for over 45 years. He and his wife, Nurkle, were missionaries in Jamaica for 13 years. They are blessed with two sons, one daughter and a granddaughter.

Winston, a former primary school headteacher in the UK, retired as principal of Midland Bible Institute (MBI), Jamaica, where he served from February 2001 to May 2013. He holds a doctoral degree in ministry (DMin) and is an honorary doctor of Divinity.

To my beloved wife, Nurkle, "bone of my bones and flesh of my flesh" since 27th September 1969. You are a true inspirer, encourager and motivator to me.

To the children from my loins, Philip, Faith and Andrew, who trusted the Lord in their childhood days and have continued to walk in His ways during their adult life.

To Ann-Marie and Sandra, my daughters-in-law who are women of God.

To my one and only granddaughter, Leandra, who is also saved and growing in the knowledge of the Lord.

Winston G Litchmore

CHRISTIAN EXPERIENCES & SPIRITUAL GROWTH

AUSTIN MACAULEY PUBLISHERS™
LONDON * CAMBRIDGE * NEW YORK * SHARJAH

Copyright © Winston G Litchmore 2022

The right of Winston G Litchmore to be identified as author of this work has been asserted by the author in accordance with section 77 and 78 of the Copyright, Designs and Patents Act 1988.

All rights reserved. No part of this publication may be reproduced, stored in a retrieval system, or transmitted in any form or by any means, electronic, mechanical, photocopying, recording, or otherwise, without the prior permission of the publishers.

Any person who commits any unauthorised act in relation to this publication may be liable to criminal prosecution and civil claims for damages.

Unless otherwise stated, biblical quotations and references are: Scriptures taken from the New King James Version. Copyright © 1979, 1980, 1982 by Thomas Nelson, Inc. Used by permission. All rights reserved.

Scripture quotations from the Authorised Version and marked KJV are reproduced in accordance with Cambridge University Press permission request guidelines.

A CIP catalogue record for this title is available from the British Library.

ISBN 9781398467897 (Paperback)
ISBN 9781398467903 (ePub e-book)

www.austinmacauley.com

First Published 2022
Austin Macauley Publishers Ltd®
1 Canada Square
Canary Wharf
London
E14 5AA

My beloved wife, Nurkle, and my daughter, Faith, who are my daily prayer partners have been initial editors and proofreaders of the manuscript.

Philip, my elder son, wrote the words and music for the song "You Must Be Washed" when he was at the tender age of 12.

Andrew, my younger son, has constantly prompted me to write a book and get it published.

George Verwer, founder of Operation Mobilisation and director of OM Special projects, who enthusiastically supported the idea of writing a book and provided advice concerning publishing.

My brother in Christ, John Bennett read the manuscript and made suggestions regarding its readiness for publication.

Thanks also to the many family members and friends who have been encouraging during the book writing process.

Table of Contents

Foreword	11
Preface	13
Introduction	15
Chapter 1 - Who Is a Christian?	19
Biblical Teaching	20
Room for Jesus	24
You Must Be Washed	26
Forgiveness and Salvation	27
The Holy Spirit Indwelling the Christian	28
Chapter 2 - Assurance of One's Salvation	31
Chapter 3 - Baptism	41
Looking Forward to My Baptism	42
The Significance of Baptism	43
Symbolic Meaning	45
Chapter 4 - Christian Fellowship	49
Chapter 5 - Separation	61
Chapter 6 - The Lord's Supper (Breaking of Bread or Communion)	73
There's a Mansion	79
Chapter 7 - The Christian and the Word of God	81
Store Up and Be Ready to Share	85
The Believer's Life Is Like an Open Bible	86
Chewing the Cud and Meditating on the Word of God	87
The Word of God and Me	91
His Word Assures Us	94
Chapter 8 - Prayer in the Life of the Christian	95
Some Types and Models of Biblical Prayers	100

Chapter 9 - The Old Nature and the New Nature	103
Chapter 10 - Some Distinguishing Qualities of a Growing Christian	109
Chapter 11 - Adjusting Your Christian Life to God	119
Lord, Not My Will	122
Chapter 12 - Love and the Christian	123
Love in Evidence	124
Love and Spiritual Gifts	126
Spiritual Gifts	126
Love in 1 Corinthians 13	128
Chapter 13 - Forgiveness and the Christian	133
Self-assessment questions on forgiveness	141
Chapter 14 - Temptation and the Christian	143
Chapter 15 - Joy and the Christian	151
Chapter 16 - Concluding Chapter	155

Foreword

Acts chapter 16 is a fascinating chapter in the Bible. It details the visit that Paul the apostle made to Philippi, an important city and colony in the Roman Empire. In that biblical account, we are told of the salvation of at least two individuals, Lydia of Thyatira and an unnamed jailor of the city.

Lydia is a wealthy businesswoman with a deep interest in religious things, a regular visitor to the place of prayer by the riverside. The jailor is a wholly different character, a man committed to his difficult and dangerous job of keeping the town's criminals secure by whatever means available. What unites the two is that they both need God's salvation. They both need to become Christians. Even the very devout businesswoman must open her heart to the Lord Jesus! For the jailor, it took an earthquake to arouse him out of physical and spiritual sleep before he believed!

But becoming a Christian was only the start – a life for Jesus Christ has only just begun. What next? A number of things can be noted. First, both sought to hear more about the Christian faith as Paul and Silas sought to teach them. Second, they were baptized as believers.

Third, changed lives were evident by their behaviour as they presented the message of the Lord Jesus to their families and servants and offered hospitality to Paul and Silas. Fourth, these two radically different individuals were united in Christian fellowship and met together with other Christians.

As you read on into this book, I trust that you will see similarities between the biblical account of Acts chapter 16 and Winston Litchmore's approach to his book. He explains what it means to be a true Christian. He has chapters on baptism, Christian fellowship, and what is entailed in living a Christian life. But there is another important detail that the book has in common with the biblical record of Paul's visit to Philippi. Luke, the writer of the Acts, is writing from first-hand experience; he was there. What makes this book of value is that Winston writes from personal experience. This is not a theoretical activity. He has proved the value and significance of the things of which he writes! As one who works alongside Winston, Nurkle and Faith Litchmore in the local Church in Nottinghamshire, I know them to be faithful and joyful Christians and of their desire that you should be also.

John Bennett
Chairman and General Editor
Precious Seed International

Preface

"What are you going to do Dr Litchmore now that you have retired?" This question was asked of my beloved wife Nurkle and me as we formally retired from our roles at the Midland Bible Institute (MBI) in 2013. We had completed 12 years' service at MBI in the land of our birth Jamaica where we were serving as missionaries. My response was that I would be writing a book. This has now become a reality.

As you read the chapters of this book and the Bible references in it, I trust that you will be challenged and blessed even as my family and I have been.

Special thanks and appreciation to my beloved wife Nurkle and our daughter Faith, my daily prayer partners, initial editors and proofreaders of the manuscript, to Philip (whose wife is Ann-Marie) our elder son who wrote the words for the song You Must Be Washed and to our younger son Andrew (whose wife is Sandra and daughter Leandra) who has constantly prompted me to get some of my writings published. Thanks also to my brother in Christ, John Bennett for suggestions regarding the appropriateness of the book for publication.

Winston G. Litchmore
Nottinghamshire, England, July 2021

Introduction

So you have an interest in this book, Christian Experiences and Spiritual Growth. Thank you for your interest. Are you seeking heart and soul satisfaction in life but so far have failed to achieve it? During the 1960s, there was a pop star who indicated in the lyrics of a song that he could get no satisfaction. Although he tried and tried, he could not feel satisfied. He and many of his contemporaries of the swinging sixties, although successful in their careers, the satisfaction through inner peace, joy and happiness had eluded them all.

You may be among the many who today are trying to get 'some satisfaction' and seeking a way to obtain it but to no avail. Pause for a moment – for whom are you living? Is it for God or for yourself?

Perhaps you have not yet met the Lord Jesus Christ. Jesus is the only way to satisfaction for the heart and soul of every human being on the planet. He removes the blockage between us and God caused by our sin. He gives new life, new desires and power to enjoy true Christian Experiences and Spiritual Growth. This includes the joy of Christian service. You must come personally to Him and ask Him for this exciting and new life if you are to obtain lasting satisfaction. You are incapable of finding heart and soul satisfaction by your own efforts. Ponder the words of the song below.

Let Jesus Take Over

1) *From day to day you rush madly about*
    You hope that your plans will quite smoothly work out.
    Success through your efforts is all you desire
    With a hope to serve Jesus before you retire.

Chorus:
    For whom are you living, for God or for self?
    Where are you going, heaven or hell?
    Stop the mad rush! And think of your soul
    Let Jesus take over and show you the way.

2) *No plan tomorrow can you guarantee*
    The Bible declares this, do try to agree.
    Repent of your sin and be ready today.
    Ask Jesus to save you, you must not delay.

3) *Discords of life may not readily cease*
    But Jesus will help you to meet them with ease.
    Look unto Him in every step of the way
    Your faith and obedience He'll amply replay.
(© Copyright 1982 by Winston G Litchmore)

Some of the sermons that I have preached over past years have been taken and integrated into various chapters of this book. It is my heart's desire and a prayer to God that you and all who read this book will receive a blessing. This is regardless of your age or stage. If you are a Christian may you be challenged, encouraged and built up in your faith to the glory of God.

You may be a 'backslider'. If this is the case, may you return to the Lord so that your weakened fellowship with God, your heavenly Father will be renewed and strengthened. May your satisfaction of heart and soul be restored with joy overflowing.

It is also desired that unbelievers (Those who are not Christians), who have an interest in a religion or in the Christian faith but have never made a commitment to Jesus Christ, the founder of Christianity, will understand their need to turn their lives over to Him and become Christians.

Perhaps you might be in this category: you may have no interest in Christianity or religion, or you may be against them. May a revelation of God's truth come to you as you read this book, and may you act upon that revelation and as a result make the decision to become a Christian.

Some of the lyrics from *MORE MUSIC* and *WORDS of 'THE LITCHMORES'* by *Winston G Litchmore* have been included in this book in order to emphasize or support the thrust or theme of a particular subject or chapter. *(Words and music for each song can be obtained from the author via the publisher.)*

The words of the song, *Room for Jesus*, (In Chapter 1) is my personal testimony in song and it was written in 1982 after I was born again in December 1966. Included in the chapter on 'Baptism', is my personal testimony 'Looking Forward to My Baptism'. This was in anticipation of my own baptism which took place in February 1967.

All biblical references are from the New King James Version (NKJV) unless otherwise stated. In some places, the word he has been used to cover for both genders. The words 'believer', 'Christian', 'child of God', 'saved person', 'saint' are interchangeable in meaning throughout this book.

Some scriptural references are repeated either for emphasis or because they bear common relevance to the different chapters where they appear in the book.

Chapter 1
Who Is a Christian?

"...And the disciples were first called Christians in Antioch" (Acts 11:26).

The answer to the question "Who is a Christian?" will vary greatly depending on whom you ask. To some, it means you were born in a Christian nation or you come from a Christian family and is a church attender. To others, it means you believe in Jesus or the religion that is based on Jesus' teachings. Yet others use the word 'Christian' to speak of a deep personal relationship between Jesus Christ and an individual. The name Christian was given to the early followers of the risen Lord Jesus Christ, and it is still used to describe followers of Christ to this day.

The word 'Christian' is used three times in the Bible and this is found in the New Testament. In each instance, it is referring to the first 'Christians' of the early church.

1) "...So it was that for a whole year they (Paul and Barnabas) assembled with the church and taught a great many people. And the disciples were first called Christians in Antioch" (Acts 11:26).

2) "Then Agrippa said to Paul, 'You almost persuade me to become a Christian'" (Acts 26:28).

3) "Yet if anyone suffers as a Christian, let him not be ashamed, but let him glorify God in this matter." (1 Peter 4:16).

Believers then were called 'Christians' to indicate that they were followers of Jesus Christ. The same term is used for the 'Christ ones' of today.

Biblical Teaching

The Bible teaches that good works do not make us acceptable to God or make us Christians. In other words, a person can live to a high moral standard, give money to feed the poor, go to church, and serve their neighbours, and yet not be a Christ follower or a Christian. Ephesians 2:8–9 says, "For it is by grace you have been saved, through faith, and not of yourselves; it is the gift of God, not by works, lest anyone should boast." We must understand the biblical teaching that salvation (Being born again) is the gift of God.

So then, nothing we do outside of Jesus Christ can make us become Christians. The service that we perform so generously and wholeheartedly, from biblical point of view are dead works but when one becomes a Christian, he is a new creation and he is in union with Christ. God now equips him to carry out His (God's) own plan of good works for his life as an individual. Once you are saved (Become a Christian), you are expected to do good works. "For we are his workmanship, created in Christ Jesus for good works, which God prepared beforehand that we should walk in them" (Ephesians 2:10). Good works is the fruit that proves that one has salvation. It is good to note that God will reward good works but not dead works.

A true Christian is a person who has accepted God's gift of salvation and placed their faith in Jesus Christ. This includes accepting Jesus' death on the cross as payment for our sins and accepting the truth that He was buried and rose again from the dead. God raised Jesus Christ from the dead (Resurrection) and received Him back into heaven (Ascension). This indicates that God was satisfied with Christ's finished and completed work as "The Lamb of God who takes away the sin of the world" (John 1:29). Jesus' resurrection is also proof of His power over sin, death, Satan and hell.

Those who are not Christians, are under the power of sin and will reap its consequences unless they repent and be converted to Christianity. People are not Christians for the following reasons:

(1) Although God's creation and their own consciences reveal to them that there is one true God, they refuse to acknowledge Him.

(2) Although they have heard the gospel, they reject Jesus Christ and the work of salvation which He accomplished at Calvary (Mark 16:16; 2 Thessalonians 1:8–9).

(3) They have not yet heard the good news of God's salvation so that they can respond to it. They will hear one day.

Thus the person who is not a Christian is firstly, out of fellowship with God his Creator and with Jesus the Saviour of the world and secondly, he is bound for a place called hell.

Jesus, who is loving and compassionate, knows that hell is a reality and a place to be shunned. He spoke much about hell and the lake of fire where people do not die but live forever in misery.

Jesus explained that any sacrifice which people can make to escape hell will be worth it all. He spoke of the hand, the foot and eye saying that it is better to go to heaven maimed without them than to go to hell (Matthew 18:7-9; Mark 9:43-48; Luke 12:5). Jesus repeatedly said that hell is a place where their worm does not die and the fire is not quenched. After His resurrection, Jesus commissioned His disciples, whom He called apostles, to evangelise the whole world as a rescue plan of salvation for all. If you are not a Christian, "Believe on the Lord Jesus Christ and you will be saved," and be on your way to heaven. Jesus who declared that knowing Him is the doorway to a special relationship with God says, "I am the way, the truth, and the life. No one comes to the Father except through Me" (John 14:6). A Christian, then, is one who has come to an understanding of the seriousness of being an enemy of God and has asked for and obtained forgiveness of sins and received a new spiritual life. In other words, a Christian is one who has been converted from their former life to Christianity.

I thought I could become a Christian 'when I'm ready' but that was not the case. I had to surrender and commit my life to Jesus and be saved (Born again) ahead of my own thoughts of doing so when I retire from my career. I became a Christian by repenting of my sins and received pardon and forgiveness through the Lord Jesus Christ.

I became a Christian on the first Saturday of December 1966. From my childhood days, I always thought about serving God but did not understand that I had to surrender my life to Him. Trying to enjoy the pleasures of the world did not bring joy and happiness within my heart because God was left out of my life. Although I read in the Bible about the dangers of storing treasures on earth and not giving God first place in my life, it meant nothing to me. This is because my pride and self-confidence hindered me from humbling myself and admitting that I was a sinner who needed to be saved. In one instance during my mid-teens, I completed a biblical course and gained distinction in the results but I was at enmity with the God of the Bible.

I remember my struggle to be saved in my own way and time. When life seemed hopeless and joyless, these words from the Bible came to me in my bed, "It is hard for thee to kick against the pricks" (Acts 9:5 KJV), in other words, "It is hard to fight against God". The Holy Spirit of God had convicted me of my sins and there was nothing I could do but to surrender and ask God to forgive me of my sins. This He did and gave me new life through Jesus Christ. Life no longer seemed hopeless and the cares of the world no longer rested on my mind.

I now worship and serve God, my heavenly Father, through His Son, the Lord Jesus Christ and I know there is a place reserved in heaven for me. Some 16 years after my conversion and a new way of living, I was inspired to write the song below.

Room for Jesus

1) *Long ago my heart was steeped in sin*
   Fear, torment and dissatisfaction anchored within.
   No room for Jesus, and how could there be
   When only life's problems mattered to me.

2) *Things divine were not amongst my goals*
   I was always lured by the tempter, who ruins bodies and souls.
   Life then was restless, as waves of the sea
   The life without Jesus, never is free.

3) *Suddenly I looked to God for help*
   Read His word and said many prayers, all for myself.
   There was no answer, and how could there be?
   When Christ did not really matter to me.

4) *God in due time, spoke through His living word*
   Showing that His Son died to save me from all my sin.
   I was to give Him a place in my life
   And He would then give me new life within.

5) *God is merciful, He waited patiently*
'til I bowed to Him in repentance asking forgiveness.
Jesus then answered, He heeded my prayer
I claimed Him as Saviour, Master and Friend.

6) *Jesus died to save us all from sin*
He is now alive and in heaven; He'll come again.
Make room for Jesus, now give Him your heart
You'll be in His presence and ne'er depart.
(© Copyright 1982 by Winston G Litchmore)

Those of us who know that our sins have been forgiven have peace and joy in our hearts although we have challenges in this life. The Lord Jesus is the one who helps us in our life's challenges; we have been 'born again' and are Christians.

If you are finding it difficult to understand that in order to become a Christian you must be born again and become a new creation, you are not alone.

In the Bible (John 3:1–21), we have on record the story about a most religious and moral person named Nicodemus. The story of Nicodemus shows and explains the absolute necessity for him and everyone else to be born again if they are to enter the Kingdom of God. For example, in verses three and five respectively, we read that "Except a man be born again, he cannot see the Kingdom of God" and "Except a man be born of water and of the Spirit, he cannot enter the Kingdom of God" (John 3:3 and 5). To be born again is one of the greatest miracles experienced by humanity. Jesus said to

Nicodemus, "Do not marvel that I said to you, 'You must be born again.'" (John 3:7).

You Must Be Washed

1) *You must be washed in the blood of the Lamb,*
   The one who came down from heaven to save man.
   He is the one who you should trust
   The one on whom you can depend;
   You must be washed in the blood of the Lamb.

2) *You must repent of the sins in your life.*
   The Lord will help you through all of your strife.
   You must admit that you've been wrong,
   That you've sinning all along,
   You must be washed in the blood of the Lamb.

3) *When He's allowed to come into your heart*
   You'll find the peace that He can there impart.
   You'll see that Jesus is the One
   On whom you really can depend
   You'll know that His love has never an end.
           (© Copyright 1982 by Philip G Litchmore)

Remember, when you repent of your sins (Turn from your sins) and ask God for forgiveness, and receive Jesus Christ into your life you will be born again; you will become a Christian.

Forgiveness and Salvation

The Old and New Testaments clearly and openly portray all human beings as sinners who fall short of God's standards or requirements and wilfully violate them. As sinners, human beings are alienated (Cut off, at a distance) from God and hostile to Him. The following Scriptures are very helpful:

- "For if when we were enemies, we were reconciled to God through the death of His Son, much more, having been reconciled, we shall be saved by His life" (Romans 5:10)

- "And you, who once were alienated and enemies in your mind by wicked works, yet now He has reconciled (Colossians 1:21)."

Before a right relationship with God can be established, the sin which caused alienation must be dealt with. Again both Old and New Testaments agree:

1) God is willing to forgive because of His love for us. Note and ponder Daniel's prayer to God for the people in Daniel chapter nine. Note well these words: "For we do not present our supplications before You because of our righteous deeds, but because of Your great mercies" (Daniel 9:18b).

2) God's forgiveness is associated with sacrifice. The sacrifices of atonement in the Old Testament prefigured Christ's ultimate sacrifice of Himself which is confirmed in the New Testament "in whom we have redemption through His blood, the forgiveness of sins" (Colossians 1:14). God's forgiveness is received by faith. There is nothing that human beings can do to merit forgiveness. We can only gladly receive by faith that which God offers us as a free gift (Ephesians 2:8–10).

Find and read the following Scriptures from the Bible: John 3:16; Romans 5:8; Romans 6:23; Romans 10:1–13. The Bible teaches that God the Holy Spirit takes up His dwelling place in the heart and life of the new Christian and lives there forever. You are then sealed by the Holy Spirit (See Ephesians 4:30). So then, everyone who is born again has the Holy Spirit living within him forever. "Now if anyone does not have the Spirit of Christ, he is not His" (Romans 8:9).

The Holy Spirit Indwelling the Christian

When the Holy Spirit seals Christians, this shows ownership and eternal security through Christ, which no one or no circumstances can take away. This reminds the Christian that he is no longer his own but belongs to Christ and can never be lost. The Holy Spirit is our Guarantor; He guarantees that the Christian's salvation is complete. He preserves and helps the Christian to live and grow more and more like Christ.

John chapters 14, 15 and 16 record the promise of the Holy Spirit by the Lord Jesus Christ as He comforted His disciples (Whom He called apostles) prior to His death, resurrection and return to heaven. The Lord's promise of sending the Holy Spirit was fulfilled on the Day of Pentecost when the Spirit came and indwelt the apostles who were gathered with others in Jerusalem (Acts 2:1–4). Jesus said that the Holy Spirit is the Comforter and that the Comforter will glorify God and guide us into all God's truths and help us to learn and remember them.

It is worth noting that one of the ministries of the Holy Spirit is to reproduce Christ in every believer. When the Holy Spirit is given absolute control of a believer's life, the Spirit will develop certain virtues or graces known as 'the fruit of the Spirit'. As branches bear fruit by receiving life and sustenance from the vine, so believers bear spiritual fruit by abiding in the Lord Jesus Christ. Jesus says, "I am the vine, you are the branches. He who abides in Me, and I in him, bears much fruit; for without Me you can do nothing" (John 15:5).

As a Christian, I should have ongoing fellowship with God, my heavenly Father. If I am maintaining fellowship with God, and abiding in God's Son, Jesus Christ, then I will seek to walk as Jesus walked (1 John 2:6) by displaying the fruit of God, the Holy Spirit, which is, "love, joy, peace, longsuffering, kindness, goodness, faithfulness, gentleness, self-control" (Galatians 5:22–23). Which of the nine segments or slices of the fruit of the Holy Spirit are evidenced in your life? Which of them do you want the Holy Spirit to make evident in you?

When one becomes a Christian it is most important and necessary to follow up on one's commitment by doing the following:

- Tell someone else about your new faith in Christ.
- Spend time with God each day. It does not have to be a long period of time. Just develop the daily habit of praying to Him and reading His Word. Ask God to increase your faith in Him and your understanding of the Bible.
- Get baptized as commanded by Christ.
- Seek fellowship with other followers of Jesus. The early Christians did that.
- Develop a group of believing friends to answer your questions and support you.
- Find a local church where you can worship and serve God with other like-minded Christians.

These actions will be in line with the Scriptures as you learn to be guided by the Holy Spirit who also assures the Christian that he is truly saved and can never be lost.

Chapter 2
Assurance of One's Salvation

"These things I have written to you who believe in the name of
the Son of God, that you may know that you have eternal life,
and that you may continue to believe in the name of the Son of
God" (1 John 5:13).

From a spiritual point of view, when we speak of assurance we mean full restful confidence in God's salvation through faith in Jesus Christ as Saviour.

We all have an enemy, Satan, who will make us doubt our salvation or try to weaken our faith in an unfailing God. The Bible makes it clear that everlasting life is a gift from God, given to those who receive His Son, Jesus Christ as their Saviour (John 3:16; Ephesians 2:8). The gift of everlasting life once given will never be withdrawn no matter what the circumstances may be (John 5:24).

In John 10:11-16 and 27-30, Jesus describes Himself as the 'Good Shepherd' and His followers (Those who are Christians) as sheep. The Christian is eternally saved and cannot be lost. However, the Christian cannot keep himself because he is no match for Satan. The Christian has double security in God and in the Lord Jesus Christ.

John 10:28 explains that Jesus holds him firmly and verse 29 of the same chapter explains that God also holds the believer firmly.

The Christian has assurance by the WORD OF GOD; 1 John 5:13, the WORK OF CHRIST which is complete, John 5:24, John 10:28, the WITNESS OF THE HOLY SPIRIT who indwells every believer forever, Romans 8:9, Romans 8:15–16, 1 John 5:10–11.

Assurance of salvation does not come by feelings or by how many good deeds one did in the past or present time. One cannot depend on one's feelings or good works to know that one is saved. Feelings are changeable and unreliable and so are deeds! The faithful word of God is unchangeable and totally reliable. It will ensure peace of mind and heart when the individual rests in faith upon it (Ephesians 2:8–9, Titus 3:5). The finished work of Christ assures one's salvation and the forgiveness of all sins; past, present and future when one becomes a believer.

- The Holy Spirit witnesses to us that we are saved; we are God's children. He will not lead us astray but will lead us into all truth. (Romans 8:9, Romans 8:15–16, John 14:17).
- The child of God may grieve the Holy Spirit (Ephesians 4:30) or quench Him (1 Thessalonians 5:19) but no New Testament Scripture teaches that the Holy Spirit ever leaves a child of God or that the child of God can lose his place in the family of God. Rather, we are assured that the Holy Spirit never leaves us (John 14:17, Ephesians 4:30).

- Always be conscious that you are saved, that you know that you know this fact, whoever believes in the Son of God has the witness in himself. (1 John 5:10–11). You are saved from the penalty of sin; being saved from the power of sin, and will one day be saved from the very presence of sin when the Lord returns to take believers away from this wicked world.
- If doubts arise in your thoughts, read the Scriptures which were written: "to you who believe in the name of the Son of God, that you may know that you have eternal life and that you may continue to believe in the name of the Son of God" (1 John 5:13). The Holy Spirit counsels us with the truth of the Scriptures and this does remove doubts and any fears we may have.
- You are saved forever – you cannot be saved today and be lost tomorrow (John 3:16, John 5:24, John 6:40, John 10:28). However, being saved forever does not mean that you should live carelessly. You should live to please God and shine out before humankind. Such a life and lifestyle will bring glory to God (Matthew 5:14–16, Ephesians 5:8).

Sweet and close fellowship with other Christians gives joy and satisfaction to believers as they walk with Jesus Christ consistently. Worshipping, attending Bible Readings or Bible Lectures, conversing and working with fellow believers in one's local church can provide confirmation to what you already know that you are saved.

Remember you are saved once and forever saved. The Christian's salvation is complete on the ground of the death and resurrection of Jesus Christ. Jesus died once on the cross to save sinners. God raised Him from the dead and received Him back into heaven indicating His (God's) satisfaction with Christ's finished and completed work. Jesus is "The Lamb of God who takes away the sin of the world" (John 1:29). Nothing can be added and nothing can be taken away from this great work and nothing can and will ever separate you from the love of God our heavenly Father. Romans chapter 8 and Colossians chapter 2 are challenging and encouraging passages of Scripture for you if you are in doubt about your salvation.

Romans chapter 8 begins with "no condemnation" and ends with "no separation" (Romans 8:1 and 39). It gives great joy and satisfaction as well as unspeakable comfort to all who are in Christ to know that no condemnation remains to us. The Christian having been delivered from the penalty of sin learns that his security rests upon the once and for all finished work of Jesus Christ. He is also inspired by the fact that his Lord and Saviour is in heaven interceding for him and all other believers (Romans 8:34). The security against the power of sin is the present work of the Holy Spirit within the believer and we overcome through our faith in God and His Word (1 John 5:4). The Holy Spirit also makes intercession for believers (Romans 8:26). What blessed assurance! The Lord Jesus Christ and the Holy Spirit make intercession for believers. This fact is of enormous encouragement and peace of mind especially when our faith in the Lord is being tested through trials and other difficulties.

In Colossians Chapter 2, the apostle Paul was concerned for the spiritual stability of the Colossian

Christians. Paul wanted them to know that he was praying for them although he had not met them face to face. He encouraged them in their faith and in their love and unity in Christ. He warned them about enticement to sin and against an error which could undermine their faith and belief in Christ's finished work and their complete salvation. The apostle told them, and this applies to every Christian today: "Beware lest anyone cheat you through philosophy and empty deceit, according to the tradition of men, according to the basic principles of the world, and not according to Christ" (Colossians 2:8). It is most important to note that Paul did not call their salvation into question since that was intact but was concerned that they were not made to stumble in their walk (Manner of living as Christians).

From Paul's letter to the Colossians, the believer, therefore, should walk forward and not backwards.

• Walk as he has received the Lord Jesus Christ (Colossians 2:6). It is important to place the highest value on one's conversion and walk by faith in the wonder of Christ's love. As Lord and as Head of the Church, He is not only enough for now but for the whole Christian life.

• Walk rooted in Christ, "Rooted and built up in Him" (Colossians 2:7). Be like the roots of a tree, reaching out to take in water and absorbing nutrients for growth from the ground. All that one needs is found in Christ (Colossians 2:8–9), not in philosophy but in faith, not in the world but in the word of God. The more the believer loves Christ is the more Christ reveals Himself to him. The more Christ reveals Himself to the believer is the

less likely he is to be led away by false teaching.
- Walk refreshed in Christ Jesus the Lord, "as you have been taught" (Colossians 2:7).
- Walk rejoicing in the Lord, "Abounding in it with thanksgiving" (Colossians 2:7). As he ponders the great salvation in Christ and overflows with praise and gratitude to God, this is an antidote against false teachings.
- Colossians 2:10 tells us that we are complete in Christ. The believer should therefore keep looking to Him and trusting in His word. That completeness is in the all-sufficient Lord Jesus Christ who provides us with all that is needed in terms of life and of godliness.

As a Christian you should:
- ***Know*** who Jesus is; Colossians 2: 3 and 9 (See also Matthew 16:13–16). Christ is deity. He is God and all knowledge and resources are in Him and no one else.
- ***Know*** what Jesus has done for you; Colossians 2:13 and 15. By His death, burial and resurrection, Christians are new creatures in Christ and with Christ. He has freed us from the curse of the law and its rituals. He has conquered all evil powers and has removed the need to be in fear of them.
- ***Know*** who you are as a Christian; Colossians 2:10 and 12. You are complete in Christ. You belong to Him by His own complete work within you. He did this without the law and without any human merit.
- ***Know*** what you are to do for Him; Colossians 2:6 and 7. Walk in Christ's love and obey the truth that you have been taught from the Scriptures. Exercise faith in Jesus as Lord and live a life of faith and thanksgiving.

Ponder the words of the apostle Paul to Titus: "They profess that they know God but in works they deny him, being abominable and disobedient, and unto every good work reprobate" (Titus 1:16). Jesus left us a perfect example by living what He taught completely. Acts 1:1 tells us about what Jesus did; "both to do and teach". The apostle John, in 1 John 2:6, exhorts that if we say that we abide in Jesus, we should walk as He walked.

As stated above, we are complete in Christ, and when He returns for us (Christians) He will present us faultless to His Father. Here on earth, however, we grow from infants (Baby Christians) to full-grown (Mature) Christians as we obediently carry out the goals and assignments which He sets for us (Romans 12:1–2). It is important to note that the Bible does not teach 'sinless perfection' for believers, since believers do sin on their Christian journey. It teaches that believers should be faithful in obeying the will of God for their individual lives.

When considering the assurance of your salvation, checking the quality of your daily life against the word of God can be helpful. The contents in the tables below are noteworthy.

Check	Scripture Reference
1). As to whether the Christian possesses the right belief concerning the Lord Jesus Christ. A Christian who has the right belief confesses that: - Jesus is the Christ - Jesus is the Son of God - Jesus came in the flesh. - Jesus is Lord	1 John 5:13 John 20:30 1 John 2:22 1 John 4:2 Romans 10:9
2). As to whether the Christian's life is marked by righteous conduct (Living right). Righteous conduct includes: - Walking in the light. - Obedience to the word of God. - The desire to live as Jesus lived	1 John 2:29 1 John 3:10 1 John 1:7 1 John 3:24 1 John 2:6

3). As to whether the Christian loves other Christians and wants to be in their company.	1 John 3:10–18 1 John 4:7–8, 11–12, 20–21
A Christian who is in a backslidden state will have little or no desire to be closely associated with spiritual Christians and seldom attends church meetings, and may seek to hide his problems. However, in such instances, the solution is to read God's Word, pray earnestly, take your problem to the Lord and firm up a relationship with believers and attend church meetings more often even than before.	
Note how the believers of the early church were together in the same place daily.	Acts 2:44–47
Believers of today should endeavour to meet together as often as possible.	Hebrews 10:23–25

Results of Assurance of One's Salvation	Scripture Reference
Joy; a deep-seated contentment and satisfaction of sins forgiven	1 Peter 1:8 1 John 1:7
The banishment of unworthy fear of God	1 John 4:17–19
Confidence in God and boldness before Him with reverence for Him.	1 John 3:19–22 1 John 5:14–15
The avoidance and hatred of sin alongside the love for sinners.	1 John 2:1
The knowledge to know that if a Christian sins he does not lose his salvation	1 John 1:9 John 10:28–30 John 5:24
A looking forward to being with our Lord Jesus Christ	Titus 2:13 2 Timothy 1:12

In order to know more about the Lord Jesus Christ and to live a life pleasing to Him, the Christian must thoroughly acquaint himself with the word of God which is in His book the Bible. His word is truth and a right understanding of it helps us to do what is right going forward, such as the next step that one should normally take on becoming a Christian. In our next chapter, we will consider the scriptural precept and practice of baptism.

Chapter 3
Baptism

*"Then those who gladly received his word were baptized; and
that day about three thousand souls were added to the church"
(Acts 2:41).*

According to biblical New Testament principles, once you are born again you should then be baptised. In Acts chapter two, we read that on the Day of Pentecost the apostle Peter was preaching a sermon to a great crowd who had gathered in Jerusalem. On being asked by those who were convicted of their sins as to what they should do to be saved, Peter told them that they should repent and then be baptised.

As before mentioned, I was born again in December 1966. The following is the testimony that I wrote on Saturday 25 February 1967 (The night before I was baptised) to be read before entering the baptismal pool. I was baptised on Sunday 26 February 1967.

Looking Forward to My Baptism

"Therefore if any man be in Christ, he is a new creature: old things are passed away; behold, all things are become new" (2 Corinthians 5:17 KJV). Since my conversion, I can see and realise that my whole life has been transformed.

Looking back on the hour when I heeded the voice of my Saviour, I now remember my first true prayer to God. In it I prayed for forgiveness of sins, courage to make it known to all that Jesus Christ had called me to repentance and that I had heeded His voice. By myself, this would not have been possible but with the Spirit of God urging me to tell of the good news, I have endeavoured to make Him known. I have prayed earnestly, and with my supplications unto God, I am happy to say that my prayers for strength, courage, wisdom, knowledge and understanding, have left me without a shadow of doubt concerning the things that God can do.

It is with a well-made up mind and a heart ringing with the bells of joy, that I wait upon tomorrow to be baptised in the name of the Father, the Son and the Holy Ghost. Though the pathway will be rough and dreary at times, I know that there is an anchor to keep my soul safe and sure while the billows roll. Such is Christ my Lord.

Many have told me that as soon as I have been baptised I will then go on for three or four weeks and return to worldly ways. One thing is clear in my mind, as it was, even before I was born again through God's abiding love and grace, I intend to stand fast in the liberty of Christ who has set me free (Galatians 5:1). In addition, it is my sincere desire and also my request to God our Father that no one should dissuade me from following after His Son Jesus Christ. With God's Holy Spirit in me, it is my desire to hold fast to that which is good (1 Thessalonians 5:21).

I cannot picture what my witness for Christ will be after I have been received into fellowship with His other saints. I can only pray that the burning desire which is now embedded in me will continue. If I can let the light of salvation shine as Jesus commanded in Matthew 5:16, then the glory will go to God in heaven.

The Significance of Baptism

It is generally agreed that spiritual birth and baptism are closely linked. Baptism is for the born-again Christian only. It is not sprinkling with water and is not for babies or infants. It is for those who have heard the good news of salvation, understand it and have opened their hearts to give heed to its message. They have now become Christ's property and want to express allegiance to Him. Those who are united to the Lord Jesus Christ symbolically participate in His death and resurrection, and as a result, they are changed, experiencing a transformation toward Christ's likeness (2 Corinthians 3:18).

Baptism is total immersion under water. It comes from the word 'bapto' to dip; 'baptizo', an intensive form, means to dip thoroughly. It never means to sprinkle or to pour. Baptism is an act of obedient discipleship, an act of obedience to Christ's command (Matthew 28:19).

Some biblical examples in addition to Acts 2:41 are:

- Baptism of the Ethiopian eunuch (Acts 8:36–39).
- Saul of Tarsus' (Later called Paul) baptism (Acts 9:18).
- The baptism of Lydia and her household (Acts 16:14 and 15).
- The Philippian Jailer and all his household (Acts 16:30–33).

Baptism is appointed and approved by the Lord Jesus Christ (Matthew 28:19). Baptism is commanded by the Lord Jesus for all nations once individuals have been born again (Become Christians). In Matthew 28:19-20, Jesus told His disciples, "Go therefore and make disciples of all nations, baptising them in the name of the Father and of the Son and of the Holy Spirit, teaching them to observe all things that I have commanded you…" Jesus sees it as the right thing to do and He Himself was baptised (Matt 3:13–17) although He is distinct from sinful man. Remember, Jesus knew no sin, did no sin, and in Him is no sin. He could not sin. John the Baptist thought himself unworthy to baptise the Lord but Jesus said to him, "Permit it to be so now, for thus it is fitting for us to fulfil all righteousness" (Matthew 3:15). The Living Bible, Revised British Edition, renders it this way: **"Please do it, for I must do all that is right."**

Symbolic Meaning

Baptism has an important symbolic meaning. It demonstrates publicly that one is born again and following the Lord Jesus Christ. Baptism bears testimony to the fact that the individual has new life through the power of the Holy Spirit. It is like a visual aid; symbolising Christ's death, burial and resurrection. In being baptised, the Christian is symbolically sharing in this death, burial and resurrection. "Therefore, we are buried with Him through baptism into death, that just as Christ was raised up from the dead by the glory of the Father, even so we also should walk in newness of life" (Romans 6:4).

In being submerged in the waters of baptism, the believer shows forth in figure his death and burial with Christ (Romans 6:4), his separation from the world (Colossians 2:12–20) although still in the world. "I have been crucified with Christ, it is no longer I who live but Christ lives in me and the life which I now live in the flesh I live by faith in the Son of God, who loved me and gave Himself for me" (Galatians 2:20).

In being raised up out of this symbolic grave, the Christian confesses his rising from the dead with Christ to walk in newness of life and to seek those things above. "If then you were raised with Christ, seek those things which are above, where Christ is sitting on the right hand of God" (Colossians 3:1). When the meaning of baptism becomes clear from the Scriptures, it is easy to see why Satan has persistently sought to twist the truth about baptism and supplant it by counterfeit. The death and resurrection of Christ was the defeat and utter destruction of Satan's kingdom and Satan does not like to be reminded of this.

Believers who live out the truth of baptism as a daily experience, are better able to live in victory over Satan's evil devices. As we continue to live in a sinful world, whenever we are tempted, we should remember what our baptism means (Romans 6:1–4). Every born-again person needs to understand that at the start of the Church, the normal thing was for all believers to be baptised soon after their conversion.

It is encouraging to read the story of the Ethiopian eunuch in Acts 8:36–39 and note keenly verse 36: "Now as they went down the road, they came to some water. And the eunuch said, 'See, here is water; what hinders me from being baptised?' As this story unfolds, we learn that the Ethiopian eunuch was baptised after having declared his faith in Jesus Christ as the Son of God. He continued on his journey home with rejoicing. To be born again and to be baptised are pleasing to God and cause rejoicing among other believers.

Do pay special attention to this scriptural truth: **One cannot get baptised to be born again. This is impossible. One is first born again – then baptism follows as the next stage.**

In summary:

- Baptism is a command of the Lord Jesus Christ, to be obeyed by all who are born again, not just to be pondered.
- Baptism is a public declaration of faith in Christ and of allegiance to Him.
- Every believer's baptism is a witness of the death, burial, and victorious resurrection of our Lord and Saviour Jesus Christ and brings glory to Him.
- A believer's baptism takes place once and it is completed within a few minutes. However, the Christian's walk with Christ in newness of life is to be evident for as long as the believer's life lasts on earth. Separation from the world and victory over Satan's attacks are evidences of new life in the Lord Jesus Christ.

Chapter 4
Christian Fellowship

"And they continued steadfastly in the apostles' doctrine and fellowship, in the breaking of bread, and in prayers" (Acts 2:42).

In Acts chapter two, we read that 3,000 persons responded positively to Peter's preaching and as a result were born again. They were then baptised and were united with the other believers and taught by the apostles. The desire of the new believers to be with the people of God and share things in common with them can be clearly seen from the account of Acts 2:42–47. There was a sense of being separated unto God from the world and a community of interests among them. New believers in Christ need to be with other believers where they can learn the word of God and worship God, pray, grow spiritually and become mature in the Christian faith. The fellowship of believers is unique and most practical. No other fellowship can match it.

Christians should seek to have fellowship with other Christians. We sometimes sing, "Blest be the tie that binds our hearts in Christian love, the fellowship of kindred minds is like to that above." Acts 4:32 records that believers in the early church "were of one heart and one soul, neither did anyone say that any of the things he possessed was his own but they had all things in common." Note that although they had "all things in common", the right of individual possession was not forbidden among them. In a remarkable act of Christian charity, individual believers were exercised to share their resources with others. This was completely voluntary; those who had, shared with those who lacked. Such ministry sent out the message that Christian fellowship and Christ likeness were of greater importance to them than worldly goods. Sharing is a normal practice among Christians today.

Fellowship is a partnership. It is the term used for the common sharing among Christians in the grace of God, the salvation Christ brings, and in the Holy Spirit who indwells all believers. The fellowship which Christians have with one another, therefore, springs from the fellowship they have with God the Father and with His Son Jesus Christ (1 John 1:3).

We cannot have fellowship with God and not have fellowship with our brothers and sisters in Christ. We cannot love God without loving our fellow Christians. The apostle John writes: "If someone says, 'I love God,' and hates his brother, he is a liar; for he who does not love his brother whom he has seen, how can he love God whom he has not seen?" (1 John 4:20).

Christian fellowship truly gives a sense of belonging as exemplified by the early believers and recorded in the Acts. Do you presently have this sense of belonging to a local company of believers? If not, why not? We note the action of Peter and John after they were threatened and released by those who were opposed to the apostles preaching in the name of Jesus, "And being let go, they went to their own companions and reported all that the chief priests and elders had said to them" (Acts 4:23).

One experiences fellowship when one shares life, events, commitment, trust, and understanding with other Christians. Fellowship also:

- Expresses like-mindedness – Philippians 2:1–2; Acts 4:32.
- Communicates acceptance – Galatians 2:9.
- Helps believers grow – Acts 2:42.
- Encourages the sharing of the work and the resources in the church – 2 Corinthians 8:1–5.
- Includes bad times as well as good times – Philippians 3:10, Romans 12:15 ("Rejoice with those who rejoice, and weep with those who weep.").

Every Christian should seek to fellowship with other Christians in a local gathering. This should be:

- A place where baptised believers meet.
- A place where the word of God is faithfully and rightly taught.
- A place where the word of God is practised.
- A place where Christian fellowship is enjoyed.
- A place where prayers are offered.
- A place where love is evident in the spiritual and practical sense.
- A place where spiritual gifts are developed and exercised.

In some Christian groups or gatherings known as local churches or local assemblies, it is the practice to receive other Christians – members of the body of Christ – into the company of believers gathered together in the name of the Lord Jesus Christ. In other words, the "right hand of fellowship" (Galatians 2:9) is extended so that those who are received can share in the rights and privileges as well as the responsibilities of the assembly. However, if the Christian's living is out of step with certain biblical standards, fellowship can be withheld.

In 1 Corinthians 5:9–13, the apostle Paul told the Corinthian Church that immorality must be judged, and especially if those within the fellowship are involved. There are six behavioural conducts if known and confirmed about a believer that can exclude him from being received into the fellowship of believers in a local church or cause fellowship to be withdrawn or withheld from a believer (1 Corinthians 5:11). However, a change in such behaviours, if seen and known, should lead to acceptance or restoration into membership in the future. Membership of the worldwide Church is permanent and constant. A believer belongs to it even when temporarily excluded from a local gathering.

1.) Sexual immorality – (Fornication) sexual intercourse with someone to whom you are not married; other forms of sexual immorality.
2.) Covetousness – (Greed) the passionate desire for material possessions i.e., constantly focusing one's desire on some material object, especially that which belongs to someone else.

3.) Idolatry – worship of idols, including putting anything or anyone in front of or ahead of God in one's life or lifestyle.
4.) Reviling (Railing) – slandering, showing contempt, and or, using abusive language to or about another person.
5.) Drunkenness – a state of being in a stupor due to intoxication with an alcoholic drink.
6.) Extortion – the act of trying to get money, goods, property, or anything of value from another person by threat or by using violence, or any other unlawful threat, fear or humiliation.

Where believers gather is holy because God dwells in them and moves among them and He is Holy. In writing to Timothy regarding the qualification of overseers (Bishops or elders) and deacons, the apostle Paul wrote, "…I write so that you may know how you ought to conduct yourself in the house of God, the pillar and ground of the truth" (1 Timothy 3:15). It is obvious then that purity must be maintained by the individual believer as well as among all believers within the local church fellowship. This is pleasing to God and to Jesus Christ who is the Head of the Church and to the Holy Spirit who guides the Church (The local company of believers) concerning the will of God.

In the light of what we have considered so far regarding Christian Fellowship, it will be helpful for us to explore at least two implications of Christian Fellowship. These are (a) Growth with Knowledge and (b) Practical and Personal Holiness. One other implication of Christian Fellowship is Separation and this will be dealt with in another chapter.

(a) Growth With Knowledge

It is reasonable to say that a toddler cannot be said to have fellowship with its father in wallpapering or painting a room. Zeal and enthusiasm to help may be present but the toddler lacks both strength and knowledge with understanding in room decorating. As the toddler grows in strength, and in the understanding and intelligence gained by watching his father, over time the child will have developed the skills, not only to decorate the room but to discuss its merits with his father. In 1 John 1:3, the writer who has seen and heard, and learned vital truths from the Lord Jesus is passing them on to believers. Believers can learn together, fellowship together and grow together in the precious truths of the word of God.

Some believers' usefulness to God is hampered or limited owing to spiritual or moral weakness or limited spiritual knowledge. The believer becomes strong and knowledgeable through reverent, prayerful and practical study of the word of God by individual study alone with God, by family worship in the home, through corporate Bible Study and teaching at church gatherings. The apostle Peter says, "but grow in the grace and knowledge of our Lord and Saviour Jesus Christ" (2 Peter 3:18a).

Spiritual growth is an essential aspect of the life of all believers. However, growth does not happen immediately but it requires patient endurance. The word of God plays a vital role in a believer's conversion. As he continues to feed on the word of God and draws nourishment from it along with prayer, he grows through various stages of spiritual development. Whether a new convert is a youngster, middle-aged or aged adult, he undergoes these stages. The more he gets to know God, the greater his faith in God and in the word of God will grow. Romans 10:17 tells us, "So then, faith comes by hearing, and hearing by the word of God." As he exercises this faith in an all-powerful, holy and loving God, he experiences victory over the old nature, Satan and the world systems which try to drag him downward.

The word of God is an equipping tool (2 Timothy 3:16–17). Careful study of Scripture equips believers for serving in God's work. Note that the Scripture as a thorough equipping tool provides for doctrine, reproof, correction and instruction in righteousness. This is in order that the believer may be equipped for every good work. Bible teachers and leaders in the local church gathering have the opportunity and responsibility of using the Scriptures in the laying of foundational truths, providing direction, confronting error and false teaching, correcting wrong behaviour by giving instruction in righteousness, and helping believers in their spiritual growth.

(b) Practical and Personal Holiness

The Christian is expected to live a holy life by practice or habitual action. Holiness in the practical sense is:

i. The habit of being of one mind with God, that is, according to the way we find His mind described in the Scriptures.
ii. The habit of agreeing with God's judgement.
iii. The habit of loving what God loves.
iv. The habit of hating what God hates (God loves people but He hates sin).
v. The habit of measuring things in this world by the standard of the word of God.

A Christian who lives with unconfessed sin is not living in close fellowship with God, neither can such Christian enjoy sweet fellowship with other Christians who are living to please Him. This does not mean that that one has lost his salvation. Salvation is everlasting, it lasts forever! Fellowship can be broken but can be restored. "If we say that we have fellowship with Him, and walk in darkness, we lie and do not practise the truth. But if we walk in the light, as He is in the light, we have fellowship with one another, and the blood of Jesus Christ His Son cleanses us from all sin" (1 John 1:6–7).

It is worth bearing in mind some important features of Christian Fellowship such as its universality, individuality, unity and diversity.

With regards to the *Universality of Christian fellowship*, the words of the apostle Paul can be applied: "To the church of God which is at Corinth, to those who are sanctified in Christ Jesus, called to be saints, with all who in every place call on the name of Jesus Christ our Lord, both theirs and ours" (1 Corinthians 1:2). Locality makes no difference, there are no geographical boundaries, no barriers of race or colour or language or social distinction, and no church of any particular group or country which excludes a believer from the Church. As mentioned previously, there are immoral behaviours that can exclude him from a local church gathering. However, he remains a member of the worldwide Church during his period of exclusion

Throughout the world, which is God's world, are several large, medium-sized and small groups of believers and individuals who together comprise the worldwide Church. No one believer knows for sure who all the other believers are. In other words, no one knows who all the true members of the Church are but every believer knows himself and some other believers. Some members of the true Church we will never know or speak with on a personal basis in this life. We may not even hear about them but God knows each one personally (2 Timothy 2:19, John 10:14, 27).

The *individuality of Christian fellowship* is featured in 1 Corinthians 12:13–14, 18, 20 and 27. Each one has a part to play. Every believer is evidence of God's sovereign movement and must be seen and accepted as such. Though there are many individuals in a local church, all are perfectly blended and tempered to form one body. No one member is to be inconspicuous either by the individual's absence or presence, for example, at meetings. The body is incomplete without the smallest member or the one farthest away from the head, for example, the toe. There is no unimportant Christian individual in the body of Christ.

It is important to note that while *individuality* portrays personal differences such as character as well as natural and spiritual gifts, individualism portrays doing things in your own way, or independently of members of the fellowship. Individual members should all play their part if unity and growth are to be realised in the local company of believers. This includes you and me and everyone else. The most effective way to achieve this result is to faithfully attend arranged church meetings as much as one is able and to be involved in the privileges and responsibilities of the local company.

It is true to say that some believers are temporarily hindered by sickness, legitimate duties or various disabilities. Such situations are dealt with in love and understanding and alternative arrangements can be made to include them in the meeting sessions or to provide them with recorded reports as appropriate. However, there are numerous passages of Scripture in the Bible spanning both Old and New Testaments which urge that believers attend church services as a duty and as a privilege. Note Psalm 27:4, Psalm 84:1, 4, 10, Psalm 122:1, Nehemiah 13:11, Acts 4:31. Hebrews 10:24–25 exhorts that believers fellowship with one another by being considerate toward one another, encouraging love and good works and "not forsaking the assembling of ourselves together as is the manner of some".

As an individual Christian, you grow as you spend much time with the Lord in praise, prayer and the reading of His word. If you have a family you may also hold family worship sessions at home and have a testimony in your own local community. These exercises are profitable and important but they do not replace attendance at your local church gatherings. Your regular attendance and association with God's people, send a message to others around you concerning your identity and standing in Christ. More importantly, this practice provides spiritual nourishment, joy and satisfaction and support during challenging times.

You are a part of that support system to the other believers of your local church fellowship. Never say that you are not needed and that your contribution does not account for much. The local church body of which you are a member is incomplete without you and your spiritual gift or gifts.

When we speak of the *unity of Christian fellowship*, it is profitable for us to note what the apostle Paul writes to the Corinthians concerning this matter; "But now indeed there are many members, yet one body" (1 Corinthians 12:20). There is but one body and an individual believer cannot scripturally belong to any body which is less than the 'one body'.

Unity does not mean uniformity, therefore, there is *diversity in Christian fellowship*. We all cannot do the same work. For one thing, we are not all qualified or gifted for the same task. There are many functions in the body. Question: What aspect of the Lord's work am I asked to do right now or where do I fit in the body of Christ? Obviously, the believers of Acts chapter two must have given this matter some thought and acted upon it. See Acts 2:44–45 and Acts 4:32–37.

Christians should beware of *bad fellowship*. The Bible points out the dangers of Christians, fellowshipping with wrongdoers or evildoers. "And have no fellowship with the unfruitful works of darkness but rather expose them. For it is shameful even to speak of those things which are done by them in secret" (Ephesians 5:11–12). The believer should live a life separated unto God. He lives in this world and should not indulge in the sinful practices of unbelievers. Separation from the world should figure greatly in the life of the believer. Our next chapter is on the subject of separation.

It would be remiss of me to omit the importance of ***Christian Love*** in the fellowship of saints as well as in the experiences and spiritual growth of the individual Christian. This subject will be addressed in the chapter on **Love and the Christian**.

Chapter 5
Separation

Separation means more than just 'dividing the men from the boys' or 'the women from the girls'. The apostle Paul writing under divine inspiration exhorts the believers of Corinth to "Come out from among them" (2 Corinthians 6:17). Separation is setting apart or coming apart. It involves the separation, spiritual and moral, from those persons, places, pleasures and pursuits where God is left out. Our desires should be set against them and our motives, actions and activities should be in the opposite direction to those world systems which displease God.

As we live in this world we have relatives, in-laws and friends who are unbelievers. We work alongside colleagues in our workplace and interact with neighbours and members within our communities. In our interacting with them at practical levels, we should do so in love and friendliness but we must display distinction in moral and spiritual life from unbelievers. Therefore while we display friendliness, we should refrain from friendships, including intimate friendships with them.

In 2 Corinthians 6:14–18, the apostle Paul advises the believers against forming binding relationships with unbelievers. Such relationships could weaken the Christian's commitment to the Lord Jesus Christ, as well as compromise the integrity, biblical precepts and practices of the believer. Christians should endeavour to avoid situations that could lead them to divide their loyalties and deny the lordship of Christ in their lives. Being in the world and living a life of separation unto God means more than Christians keeping a distance from unbelievers. It means that the Christians must stay close to God as they move and work among unbelievers. Separation involves avoiding entertainments that lead to sin and it also includes how we spend our time and money. It is true to say that it is not possible for Christians to separate themselves totally from all sinful influences while living in this world.

God constantly warned His *chosen people* the Israelites against intermarrying with surrounding nations because of the danger of being drawn into their ungodly way of life and worshipping their gods. God was displeased with them. He is a jealous God who was jealous for their welfare (Isaiah 52:11) and wanted to prevent them from falling into idolatry and all the wickedness that goes along with it.

The Christian should be different and be seen to be different from unbelievers. Christians should not become dissimilarly yoked with unbelievers. Righteousness and lawlessness should not be in partnership as they have nothing in common.

There are five different words found in verses 14, 15 and 16 of 2 Corinthians 6 in connection with separation. These are *Fellowship, Communion, Accord, Part* and *Agreement.*

Fellowship (Verse 14) – The word 'partner' derived from the same root as fellowship is used in Luke 5:7 and is there associated with partnership in the activity. "So they signalled to their partners in the other boat to come and help them. And they came and filled both the boats so that they began to sink." Here there is no evidence of lawlessness but an active partnership. These men had different personalities but they worked together harmoniously, keeping their eyes on the same goal until they achieved their objective and the result was huge. This event occurred in the fishing centre, around the Lake of Galilee as recorded in Luke 5:1–11. After a fruitless night at fishing, Peter in submissive obedience to Jesus, let down his net during the day and had a huge catch of fish. Because they were too heavy for the net to hold them, Peter beckoned to James and John, also fishermen, to come and assist him with his problem. They responded positively to the request. They pulled together in the same direction and brought the huge catch to land. Here, they had a fellowship in problem-solving and in successful results. They were all fishermen, having common knowledge and skills, and the same Master the Lord Jesus Christ. They had the same occupation to catch fish. Following this incident, Jesus told them that He wanted them to devote their time to bring men to Himself. They left their fishing occupation and followed Jesus.

Communion (Verse 14) – Acts 2:44 tells us that the believers were together and had all things in common; there was no mixture of light and darkness in this example. Communion denotes a very close relationship such as exists in a marriage. When two believers marry, they are together children of 'light' and God is pleased with the union. Unbelievers are children of 'darkness' and light and darkness cannot co-exist in the same place at the same time. The apostle Paul reminded the Ephesians: "For you were once darkness but now you are light in the Lord. Walk as children of light" (Ephesians 5:8). Paul was appealing to believers at Ephesus that they should avoid immorality in their living. Here in Ephesians 5:8, he is drawing a distinction between darkness, which they were before they were saved, and light which they have now become as believers. It is helpful to note that believers have new life in Christ (2 Corinthians 5:17) and are in union with Him. As the "light of the world", He enables us to walk as lights and expose the evil deeds of darkness. Believers should not cooperate with works of darkness but separate from them to the glory and pleasure of the Lord.

Accord (Verse 15) – The word accord, speaks of harmony with one mind. Can you imagine The Lord Jesus Christ being in harmony with the devil regarding the blood-bought Christian? Most unlikely! The devil's view certainly does not accord with the Lord's, the Holy One. The devil is also known as Belial, and Belial is a name that speaks of wickedness, or worthlessness. The people who worship him are serving idols (Deuteronomy 13:13–14 KJV). Such idolatry is an abomination to the Godhead, God the Father, God the Son and God the Holy Spirit, who is absolutely holy and pure.

As we enjoy fellowship with God the Father and with His Son Jesus Christ (1 John 1:3 and 6), our lives should accord with holiness and purity. By the dedicated study of the Scriptures, prayer and the close relationship with other believers, the indwelling Holy Spirit enables us to demonstrate total allegiance to Christ. God is pleased with His people when we thus conduct ourselves. It glorifies Him and has a powerful impact on unbelievers.

The Early Church left us a good example of what it is to be in one accord with the saints in our daily lives. From Acts 2:46, we learn that the life and character of the Early Church were that of a community that was on one accord which continued daily in praising God in love and in generosity. This testimony of like-mindedness and solidarity among believers impacted unbelievers, thousands of whom responded positively by believing the gospel message that the apostles preached. These new believers were then baptised and became part of the Christian community. Acts 4:23–32 records that when persecution arose and Peter and John were released from prison, they gathered with 'their own companions' the Church. They were on one accord, "of one heart and one soul". They glorified God and prayed and as a result, the place where they assembled was shaken as God responded to their prayers.

The believers were clear and conscious that they were God's children, called by Him and set apart for His service, and they demonstrated this in practice. They had the same understanding of God and His Word, the same will and focus to serve Him, and the same love and affection towards one another. They knew that they belong together. Such united occupation by the believers with the one true God who is supreme is in direct discord with Belial, his attributes and his followers. "For all the gods of the people are idols but the Lord made the heavens" (1 Chronicles 16:26).

It is worth noting the apostle Paul's exhortation to the Corinthians: "For even if there are so-called gods, whether in heaven or on earth (As there are many gods and many lords), yet for us, there is one God, the Father, of whom are all things and we for Him and one Lord Jesus Christ, through whom are all things, and through whom we live" (1 Corinthians 8:5–6). It is profitable to examine ourselves individually to see if our life and lifestyle are in conformity in any way to those of the wicked and the lawless in whose hearts God has no place. Such examination should compel us to make the necessary adjustments when necessary. We have the help of the Holy Spirit to help us accomplish this.

Part (Verse 15) – 'Part' or 'share' means that there is acceptance or appreciation of the same things. The believer has been born again by believing in the Lord Jesus Christ and studies and practises the word of God. What fellowship can the believer have with one who does not know or believe in the believer's Saviour or in God's holy word? The answer is, none! Believers and unbelievers operate on different moral principles and have different goals and destinations. Such association is known as an unequal yoke and mars the believer's testimony.

We note again how the apostle Paul challenged the Corinthians by asking, "Or what part hath he that believeth with an infidel?" (2 Corinthians 6:15b KJV). An infidel is a person who has no religion or whose religion is not that of the majority. A person who does not subscribe to a faith or even a religion cannot please God and is perishing until he believes and embraces the gospel. From John 3:16, we understand that whoever believes in Christ will have everlasting life. Since Christ died for all including the infidel through to the self-righteous, we should pray that unbelievers everywhere will heed the gospel message and be converted unto Him. A life of separation from ungodly practices including the refusal to be part of an ungodly association, serves as a powerful message to the unbelieving world and an example to other believers.

As Christians, we should be ambassadors for Christ in our own homes and amongst our family members. Ponder the following questions:

1.) What happens if a sibling with whom you live, for example, is an infidel (An unbeliever) and wants both of you to join together to set up a business. Should you be part of the business?
2.) What should be your action or reaction?

Consider the following suggestions:

- Firstly, pray to the Lord for guidance. Ask Him for a response which will glorify Him.
- Show love to your sibling and family members on a daily basis. The believer can do this because the Lord has poured out His love in abundance in his heart by the indwelling Holy Spirit (Romans 5:5) Jesus in Matthew 5:43–48 commanded His disciples to love everyone even their enemies. As a Christian, you should love and operate in love regarding those near and far and around you.
- Demonstrate respect for your sibling, listen carefully to proposals and pass on genuine encouragement about the merits of the proposals if there are merits.
- Explain courteously and politely why you will not be able to share in the proposed business and mention any other ways in which you can help as a family member. The question, "Can two walk together, unless they are agreed?"

(Amos 3:3) should be borne in mind and answered by you.
- Speak and live the truth of God's Word consistently and continue to pray for wise and understanding behaviour on your part whatever the final decision and whatever the outcome.
- Be prepared to ask other believers or a Christian friend to assist you by praying with you that God's will be done in the matter.
- Remember, be not unequally yoked with unbelievers but be yoked to the Lord Jesus Christ. His yoke is easy and His burden is light (Matthew 11:30).

If you find yourself in the league or in partnership with any unbelievers, then you need to heed the word of God to turn away from such practice. Ask the Lord for pardon and for guidance to cease for all time.

Agreement (Verse 16) – This implies consent. The word 'agreement' brings to a climax the four previous words that the apostle Paul uses to express sinful union between believers, who are children of God, and unbelievers who are children of the devil. The word also suggests a sympathetic union of mind and will in a mutually agreed plan, which should exist only between you and other believers and the Lord.

For all believers, the criteria for any agreement with anyone should be in line with the word of God and with the principles which glorify and please God. God's standards for Christian living are set out in His inspired Word and are the most dependable and reliable of all truths. All truths are of God and Jesus spoke to the Jews concerning the freedom that truth brings to those who believe. He also told them that Satan is a liar and the father of lies (John 8:44b).

The Holy Spirit who is the Spirit of Truth dwells in all believers whose bodies are temples of God (1 Corinthians 6:19). The local church comprised of believers is also God's temple where the Holy Spirit is present and where He leads, guides and works in and among believers (1 Corinthians 3:16–17). Holiness is one of the hallmarks of a life that is filled with the Holy Spirit and obedient to the word of God.

The apostle Paul asked the question and answers it, "And what agreement has the temple of God with idols? For you are the temple of the living God. As God has said: I will dwell in them and walk among them. I will be their God. And they shall be my people." The life of the believer whose God is the Lord, and that of the idolater who serves idols are worlds apart from each other.

Idols are false gods and are dead. They are objects and images made by the hands of mortals who bow down and worship them. While idols are not in themselves harmful, people are drawn away from the Lord to worship them and to influence others to do the same. But idols can also include things which are elevated above God and come between one's soul and God, such as money, family, fame and the famous. The focus of their worship is not God the creator but on people and things.

Paul was keen for the Corinthian Christians to display in their lives the distinguishing traits that told the world that they belong to Christ. This would glorify God and bring them joy and satisfaction and lead sinners to Christ. Therefore, in an earnest appeal to them, the apostle told the believers that they should come out from among unbelievers because they practise lawlessness, and are themselves darkness. They serve Belial and worship idols. In today's world of 'political correctness' and multi-faith society, Christians are expected to heed the Apostle Paul's exhortation and avoid being in agreement with any form of idolatry, be it explicitly or implicitly.

Chapter 6
The Lord's Supper (Breaking of Bread or Communion)

"For as often as you eat this bread and drink this cup, you proclaim the Lord's death till He come" (1 Corinthians 11:26).

There are four biblical accounts of the institution of the Lord's Supper, Breaking of Bread or Communion. These are:

i. Matthew 26:26–29
ii. Mark 14:22–25
iii. Luke 22:19–20
iv. 1 Corinthians 11:23–26

Matthew 26:26–29	Mark 14:22–25	Luke 22:19–20	1 Corinthians 11:23–26
²⁶And as they were eating, Jesus took bread, blessed and broke it, and gave it to the disciples and said, "Take, eat; this is My body."	²²And as they were eating, Jesus took bread, blessed and broke it, and gave it to them and said, "Take, eat; this is My body."	¹⁹And He took bread, gave thanks and broke it, and gave it to them, saying, "This is My body which is given for you; do this in remembrance of Me."	²³For I received from the Lord that which I also delivered to you: that the Lord Jesus on the same night in which He was betrayed took bread;²⁴and when He had given thanks, He broke it and said, "Take, eat; This is My body which was broken for you; do this in remembrance of Me."

[27]Then He took the cup, and gave thanks, and gave it to them, saying, "Drink from it, all of you. [28]For this is My blood of the new covenant, which is shed for many for the remission of sins.	[23]Then He took the cup, and when He had given thanks He gave it to them, and they all drank from it. [24]And He said to them, "This is My blood of the new covenant, which is shed for many.	[20]Likewise He also took the cup after supper, saying, "This cup is the new covenant in My blood, which is shed for you."	[25]In the same manner He also took the cup after supper, saying: "This cup is the new covenant in My blood. This do, as often as you drink it, in remembrance of Me."
[29]But I say to you, I will not drink of this fruit of the vine from now on until that day when I drink it new with you in My Father's kingdom."	[25]Assuredly, I say to you, I will no longer drink of the fruit of the vine until that day when I drink it new in the kingdom of God."		[26]For as often as you eat this bread and drink this cup, you proclaim the Lord's death till He comes.

During His earthly ministry, Jesus instituted two, and only two, ordinances (Religious rites) for His Church during this present age. They are Baptism and the Lord's Supper. Both of these ordinances are closely associated with Christ's death and resurrection. But there are two outstanding contrasts between these two ordinances. Baptism is a once-for-all act of obedience since our identification with Christ is never altered. However, the influence and practical manifestation of the fact of our death and resurrection with Him should be seen throughout our entire Christian life. The Lord's Supper, in contrast, is to be observed repeatedly since it is a remembrance feast. Baptism is an individual act on the part of each believer, while the Lord's Supper or the Breaking of Bread is a corporate act of the local assembly (Local body of believers) and every time we observe it, we proclaim the Lord's death and His return for the Church because it is "till He comes".

We learn from the Scriptures that the practice of the early church Christians to remember the Lord in the Breaking of Bread was held on 'the first day of the week' (Sunday); only baptised believers participated in the Breaking of Bread (Acts 20:7–11, 1 Corinthians 16:2). Note Acts 2:41–42.

When we come to break bread we should see it as a time to remember the Lord Jesus Christ and His suffering and death (1 Corinthians 11:24–25). His suffering and death are never without His resurrection. He arose triumphantly from the grave and is alive today. "In remembrance of Me" applies to both the bread and the cup of wine which are symbols of His body and blood respectively. Why is it so important to remember Christ's sufferings? It is a reminder to us:

i. of the seriousness of sin and its reward which is death (Romans 6:23a).
ii. that the One who knew no sin became sin for us (2 Corinthians 5:21).
iii. of God's love and grace (Ephesians 2:4–5).

The Breaking of Bread should keep our vision of the cross clear and our expectation of Christ's return fresh:

- Today, we walk by faith and not by sight, but when our Lord returns, then, faith will be lost in sight, "for we shall see Him as He is" (1 John 3:2).
- Today, we look at the symbols on the table of remembrance and think of the cross but when our Lord returns, then, we will look at our Saviour and think of his love.
- Today, we take the bread in our hands, but when our Lord returns, then, we will take the hand of the Bread of Life.
- Today, we share the fruit of the vine. (Mark 14:25 – "Verily I say unto you, I will drink no more of the fruit of the vine, until that day that I drink it new in the kingdom of God.") When our Lord returns, then we will share with the True Vine, our Lord Jesus Christ.

The Lord's Supper is a solemn ordinance and violation of it constitutes disobedience to the Lord Jesus who instituted it. It should be observed with reverence, love and affection for the One who loved us and gave Himself for us. In 1 Corinthians 11:23–26, the apostle Paul sets out his revelation from the Lord regarding the institution of the Lord's Supper. He then goes on to discuss its purpose, how believers should prepare themselves for it as well as how they should conduct themselves when they gather together for it.

There's a Mansion

1) There's a mansion above, where I'm longing to be
For there's One who has gone to prepare it for me.
He has promised a place to whom He has redeemed
This is in His word, it's a promise most true
His return is very near, it may be today.

2) Jesus Christ is His name, Saviour, Master and Lord
God above who came down, dwelt amongst sinful men.
He was sorely tried and rejected by some
He was mocked and jeered when He hung on the cross.
Christ the Lord paid the price for sin when He died in our stead.

3) He was laid in a tomb; He arose from the grave
Then ascended on high to our Father above.
Soon the hour will come when the Lord will return
What a joy 'twill be – we shall meet in the air.
We shall always be in His sight, always praising His name.

(© Copyright 1982 by Winston G Litchmore)

Chapter 7
The Christian and the Word of God

"All Scripture is given by inspiration of God, and is profitable for doctrine, for reproof, for correction, for instruction in righteousness, that the man of God may be complete, thoroughly equipped for every good work" (2 Timothy 3:16–17).

The word of God is essential to the growth and spiritual development of the believer. The newly saved, who is a babe in Christ is told, "As newborn babies, desire the pure milk of the word, that you may grow thereby" (1Peter 2:2). Peter also exhorts the believer to "grow in the grace, and knowledge of our Lord and Saviour Jesus Christ" (2 Peter 3:18). Therefore, we must acknowledge that the Bible as an agent of change should transform the believer and should not be changed by anyone to suit his or her own wishes or circumstances.

The Bible, God's written word, changes lives. Its message of salvation makes the most profound change but the Scriptures can also change the way we treat others. They provide a firm foundation for society with their clear teachings on institutions such as marriage, the family, and the local church or body of Christians.

But what happens when what the Bible clearly teaches is rejected? Those who reject the teachings try to change the meaning of the word of God. Instead of trying to change the word of God to fit our own ideas, let us allow the word of God to transform us. As we read the word of God and obey it, the Holy Spirit will transform us into the kind of people God wants us to be. We must not change the word of God, let the word of God change us. It does us well to ponder the utterance of Job: "I have not departed from the commandment of His lips; I have treasured the words of His mouth more than my necessary food" (Job 23:12b).

Every believer should study, or be helped to study the Bible in its entirety. Acts 2:41–42, tells us that those who gladly believed the message which they heard "continued steadfastly in the apostles' doctrine". The apostles' doctrine means the inspired teachings of the apostles, delivered orally at first having learnt from the Lord Jesus Himself. Today it is available to us in the books of the New Testament. New converts need to be discipled. Discipleship always includes Bible teaching. Jesus commissioned the apostles, "Teaching them to observe all things that I have commanded you" (Matthew 28:20a).

Profitable Bible study involves more than just opening a chapter and reading what is there. To make the most of consistent study of the Bible and gain knowledge and increased wisdom, the Christian should set aside a regular time for Bible Study, sometimes called 'quiet time'. Unless you schedule it, you may neglect it. It is important to ask God for help and understanding before you start reading. Think carefully about what you are reading because not all the Bible's treasures lie like pebbles on the surface of the seashore. To mine 'gold', you need to dig and dig deeply. Obviously, you should seek to understand what the author was saying to the first people who read the book or letter before you decide how to apply it today. And if possible, write down at least one truth or principle to be applied to your own life. Note carefully: the truth is always the truth and God's truth does not change!

You may find some parts of the Bible more interesting than others, and some parts you may not understand at all but do not get discouraged. There is enough that you will understand, and it will revolutionize you as you seek to apply it to your daily life and lifestyle. Sometimes questions are asked as to how we got the Bible.

Always remember that the Bible is inspired by God, not by man or by the Church (2 Timothy 3:16–17, 2 Peter 1:20–21). God chose and inspired the writers over a period of 1,600 years, from approximately 1500 BC to 100 AD. He has ensured its preservation and guided its dissemination so that we have it in our hands today. All over the world, Christians are translating the word of God into local languages so that all people groups can learn about the one true God and His Son Jesus Christ.

In reading and studying the Bible, it is worth spending time to ponder some contrasting subjects with their references in the Old and New Testaments.

	Old Testament		*New Testament*	
1	Creator	Gen 1:1	Redeemer	Gal 3:13
2	Satan's Victory	Gen 3:6	Satan's Defeat	Rev 20:10
3	First promise of a Redeemer	Gen 3:15	God's timing regarding promised Redeemer fulfilled	Gal 4:4-5
4	Sin's Curse	Gen 3:17-19	Sin's Remedy	John 3:16
5	Death to hold sway	Gen 3:19	Life Eternal	John 5:24
6	Bloody Sacrifices	Ex 12:3-7	Christ the Lamb	John 1:29
7	God unapproachable	Ex 19:16-25	God our Father	Matt 6:9 Heb 10:19-22
8	Law (Ten Commandments)	Ex 20:1-17	Gospel	Rom 1:16
9	Prophecy	Isa 11:1-2	Fulfilment	Acts 3:18-19
10	Paradise Lost	Gen 3:23-24	Paradise Regained	Rev 22:14

Store Up and Be Ready to Share

The Christian should diligently store up and be ready to share the word of God appropriately. Christians who love the word of God can learn from the ant. "The ants are a people not strong, yet they prepare their food in the summer" (Proverbs 30:25). There is a group of ants called 'honey ants' or 'honey pot ants' and there are around 34 different species of these ants. They all share the ability to store large amounts of nutritious liquid, especially in the larger workers known as 'repletes'.

During the rainy seasons, the honey pot ant repletes feed so much that they swell up and become like living underground refrigerators. Some can become so large that it is impossible for them to leave their nests. They take in so much nectar that they swell up until they resemble little round berries and are hardly able to move. When food and water become scarce, these ants act as 'social stomachs' and sustain the entire colony by sharing what they have stored up in their bodies.

The born-again Christian as a messenger or teacher or representative of God must fill his heart with the truths of the Scriptures. Only as one is faithful in applying the word of God to one's own life can one honestly give its nourishment, encouragement and exhortation to others. "Be diligent to present yourself approved to God, a worker who does not need to be ashamed, rightly dividing the word of truth" (2 Timothy 2:15).

The Lord told Ezekiel to eat a scroll that contained a message full of "lamentations and mourning and woe" (Ezekiel 2:10). Because he was submissive to the Lord and applied the lesson firstly to his own heart, Ezekiel could boldly present the life-giving message to all who would listen. To understand the context of the foregoing, read Ezekiel chapters two and three.

As a believer, what are you studying at the moment? You too must develop a spiritual 'social stomach' by digesting the truths of the Bible and allowing the Holy Spirit to make them a part of your life. Then, filled with God's Word, He, the Holy Spirit enables you to remember and to appropriately and effectively dispense it to others who are in need of spiritual food. The unbeliever needs the Lord Jesus who says, "I am the bread of life" (John 6:35); the believer needs building up in his or her faith, "rooted and built up in Him and established in the faith, as you have been taught, abounding in it with thanksgiving" (Colossians 2:7).

The Believer's Life Is Like an Open Bible

The life of the believer is like an open Bible and therefore the believer must consistently be opening his or her Bible. Psalm 119 is filled with praise for the power, excellence and wonder of the word of God. Here the writer has expressed commitment to live by it and share it with others.

Note verses 45–47 of Psalm 119:

- Verse 45: "And I will walk at liberty for I seek Your precepts."
- Verse 46: "I will speak of Your testimonies also before kings, and will not be ashamed."
- Verse 47: "And I will delight myself in Your commandments, which I love."

Since the believer's life is an open Bible, the believer should seek to demonstrate the love and power of the word of God, the Bible, for everyone to see. Therefore, of all the commentaries on the Scripture, good life examples are best. Christians are the only Bible the worldly person will read; we are the sinner's gospel; we are the sceptic's laughing stock.

Chewing the Cud and Meditating on the Word of God

Chewing the cud over the word of God and meditating on it is good. It is a wonderful sight, seeing cows lying in the field chewing their cuds. But what is the cud? And why do cows spend so much time chewing their cud? Cows first fill their stomachs with grass and other food and then they settle down for a good long chew. They bring their food back up from their stomachs into their mouths and chew it again. *(This is the cud!)* Then they rework what they have already eaten, assimilating its goodness and transforming it into rich creamy milk. Is it time-consuming? Yes. Is it a waste of time? Not if they want to make good rich milk.

The phrase 'chewing the cud' is a term used to describe the process of meditation. We are referring here to spiritual, scriptural meditation. The term, 'chewing the cud', means to think or talk reflectively, to think deeply.

The writer of Psalm 119 obviously did a lot of mental chewing as he read the word of God. If we follow his example of careful and prayerful scripture reading, we will:

- Be strengthened against sin (Verse 11)
- Find delight in learning more about God (Verses 15–16)
- Discover wonderful truths (Verse 18)
- Find wise counsel for daily living (Verse 24)

Meditation is more than reading the Bible and believing it. One must go further and apply Scripture to everyday life. Take time for a good long chew. To be a healthy Christian, it is best not to treat the Bible as snack food. But, the Christian can develop and have a sweet tooth for the word of God which is the Bible.

The story is told of an individual who stopped at a convenience store somewhere in Nottingham a few years ago and asked for every Mini Chocolate Roll in stock. The customer paid cash for almost 300 of the Mini Chocolate Rolls and no one bothered to ask why so many were being purchased but one person jestingly uttered, "Perhaps our friend has a craving and a sweet tooth with a great love for chocolate rolls."

The psalmist had a craving, a sweet tooth and a great love for something far more healthy than Mini Chocolate Rolls. He loved the word of God and found it 'sweeter than honey' to his taste, "How sweet are Your words to my taste. Sweeter than honey to my mouth!" (Psalm 119:103). How can we develop our spiritual taste buds so that we have a strong craving for the sweetness of the word of God? **Read the Bible, read the Word, chew the cud over it**. It may seem obvious but one must read the word of God, the Bible if one is going to learn to love it as the psalmist did. The word of God will give a 'sweet tooth' and it is satisfying.

One cannot have too much of the 'Honey-sweet word' which will not cause diabetes, obesity or tooth decay. It is believed that a well-read Bible is a sign of a well-fed soul. This belief is true if that soul is born again.

Joshua succeeded Moses as leader of the children of Israel. God promised to be with him as He was with Moses, but Joshua was told that he had to meditate on the word of God. "This Book of the Law shall not depart from your mouth but you shall meditate in it day and night that you may observe to do according to all that is written in it. For then you will make your way prosperous, and then you will have good success" (Joshua 1:8). Joshua was not to rely on his experience of serving as an assistant to Moses but he should rely upon the law which Moses wrote down and left for him and the Israelites to observe. It was not simply Moses' words but the inspired words which God gave Moses to write. God said to Joshua:

"This Book of the Law shall not depart from your mouth." Not only must the believer read the word of God and obey it but make it a part of everyday conversation whenever the opportunity presents itself.

"Meditate in it day and night." It is impossible to do so other than by reading and studying it.

"Observe to do according to all that is written in it." All of the words of God are important and there are merits in organising one's time to ensure that one does not miss out on the regular study of the Bible. The Christian is to have a totally obedient heart towards the word of God. His word is absolutely reliable. Psalm 33:4 states, "For the word of the Lord is right, and all His work is done in truth."

"For then you will make your way prosperous, and then you will have good success." This is Motivation indeed! Look at what God promised; a prosperous way and good success.

The Word of God and Me

What It Does for Me	What It Is to Me	How It Should Be Treated by Me
It revives me – "My soul clings to the dust; Revive me according to Your word" – Psalm 119:25	It is precious to me – "…by which have been given to us exceedingly great and precious promises…" – 2 Peter 1:1–4	I am to love it – "Oh, how I love Your law! It is my meditation all the day" – Psalm 119:97
It sanctifies me – "Sanctify them by Your truth. Your word is truth" – John 17:17	It is joy and rejoicing to me – "…And Your word was to me the joy and rejoicing of my heart." – Jeremiah 15:16a	I am to search it – "You search the Scriptures… and these are they which testify of Me" – John 5:39 (see also Acts 17:10–11)

It cleanses me – "How can a young man cleanse his way? By taking heed according to Your word" – Psalm 119:9; "You are already clean because of the word which I have spoken to you" – John 15:3	It is penetrating to me – "For the word of God is living and powerful, and sharper than any two-edged sword, piercing even to the division of soul and spirit, and of joints and marrow, and is a discerner of the thoughts and intents of the heart" – Hebrews 4:12	I am to feed on it "Your words were found, and I ate them" – Jeremiah 15:15a; "How sweet are Your words to my taste, Sweeter than honey to my mouth!" – Psalm 119:103
It shows me the way ahead – "Your word is a lamp to my feet And a light to my path" – Psalm 119:105	It is purifying to me – "Is not my word like a fire? says the LORD" Jeremiah 23:29a	I am to hold fast to it – "Hold fast the pattern of sound words…" 2 Timothy 1:13; "Holding fast the faithful word as he has been taught…" – Titus 1:9

As you read the Bible, know and remember that you are special to God and "that you may proclaim the praises of Him who called you out of darkness into His marvellous light" (1 Peter 2:9). All believers must therefore study the Bible to be wise, believe it to be safe and secure, and practise it to be holy. We do not know the Bible until we obey the Bible.

The word of God is also the sword of the Spirit (Ephesians 6:17b). This is a part of the Christian armour which when worn safeguards and counteracts the evils and wickedness, and the lust of the flesh.

Remember, the word of God is an equipping tool (2 Timothy 3:16–17), and careful study of the Scripture equips believers for serving in God's work. This is important because believers are saved to do good works (Ephesians 2:10), and are then equipped to do the tasks for which the Lord has called each believer. In all these things, the believer needs to work patiently and consistently, step by step with the Lord. God is the believer's heavenly Father. Jesus is Saviour and Lord and the Master of all masters as well as the believer's closest Friend. Whatever you need to know you can ask Him through prayer. He hears and answers the prayers of believers.

If you find it burdensome to read, study, and meditate upon the word of God, you should pray that this exercise will become a delight. Having fellowship with other believers who are like-minded in studying and sharing the word of God can be most helpful. However, knowledge of the word of God should be displayed in your daily living and this should include a firm allegiance to Christ.

His Word Assures Us

1) When I rise in the morning I will lift my thoughts to the Lord.
With my heart and my voice I will praise His glorious name.
Praise the Lord in the morning for His goodness
His loving kindness is ever the same
For His word does assure us that we're precious in His sight.

2) At my work in the daytime, I'll gladly do all my tasks.
With the greatest of effort I'll endeavour to succeed.
Praise the Lord in the daytime for His goodness.
He gives us strength every hour of each day
And His word does assure us that He helps us on our way.

3) As the evening approaches, I'll have worked and also have played.
Whether happy or sad I will thank Him with gladness of heart.
Praise the Lord in the night-time for His goodness
However tired or weary you are
For His word does assure us that we're always in His care.

(© Copyright 1983 by Winston G Litchmore)

Although we read and study the Bible and meditate on God's word, the Christian should not forget to pray. This is vital in seeking to live and maintain Christian growth.

Chapter 8
Prayer in the Life of the Christian

"And they continued steadfastly in the apostles' doctrine and
fellowship, in the breaking of bread, and in prayers"
(Acts 2:42)

"Pray without ceasing" (1 Thessalonians 5:17).

Prayer has a strong bearing on one's life as a follower of Jesus Christ. Prayer is one of the master keys to the victorious Christian life. There is no greater joy than to unload the burden of one's mind at the feet of Jesus in prayer. 1 Thessalonians 5:17 exhorts us to pray at all times while Colossians 4:2 encourages us to keep praying and watch for the answers at the same time giving thanks. **Thanksgiving and praise** to God should be included in prayer. God is worthy of our continual praises because of who He is and worthy of thanksgiving because of what He does for us.

It must always be kept in mind that prayer is communicating with God. It is not 'listen Lord for your servant is speaking'. Prayer is not speaking to a god of wood and stone, or to a god that cannot save (Isaiah 45:20) but to the God who can save and hear (Isaiah 59:1). When we pray, we should not seek to conquer God's reluctance but lay hold of His will.

There is indeed the need for humankind to pray. The first indication in the Bible concerning prayer is found in the last part of the last verse of Genesis chapter 4: "Then men began to call on the name of the Lord" (Genesis 4:26).

The greatest example regarding prayer is the Lord Jesus Christ. He is our perfect example and Luke's Gospel records seven examples concerning Jesus and prayer:

i. Luke 3:21 – When Jesus prayed the heaven was opened.
ii. Luke 5:16 – Jesus often withdrew Himself from the crowd to pray. (Verse 15 is the key.)
iii. Luke 6:12–13 – Jesus prayed all night in prayer to God before choosing His disciples, whom He also named apostles.
iv. Luke 9:29 – On the Mount of Transfiguration the appearance of His face was altered and His robe became white and glistening as He prayed.
v. Luke 11:1–4 – When Jesus' disciples heard Him pray, they requested, "Lord teach us to pray, as John taught his disciples." Jesus taught them a model prayer (Commonly called the Lord's Prayer).
vi. Luke 22:32 – Jesus confirmed to Peter that He had prayed for him. Jesus had a special concern for him and He knew the failure which was about to overtake Peter because of Peter's over-confidence in himself. The Lord interceded for Peter; the Lord intercedes for us today in heaven as our Great High Priest.

vii. Luke 23:34 – Jesus asked God to forgive His persecutors while He was on the cross. He said, "Father forgive them, for they know not what they do."

Recognising that Jesus is our perfect example in prayer, how should we pray? The word fervently means to be ardent, zealous, warm in feeling and earnestly means sincerely, seriously. Note the following:

- Luke 22:44 – This verse speaks of our Lord Jesus. "And being in agony, He prayed more earnestly. Then His sweat became like great drops of blood falling down to the ground." It is also worth noting the Lord's own prayer to His Father in John 17. Jesus prayed for His disciples and for all believers.
- Colossians 4:12 – "Epaphras…always labouring fervently for you in prayers."
- James 5:16b – "The effective fervent prayer of a righteous man avails much."
- James 5:17–18 – Elijah prayed earnestly and his prayers were answered.

When we pray, we should pray reverently, remembering who God is; God is Holy. In Matthew 6:9, the Lord Jesus in teaching His disciples the 'model' prayer said to them, "In this manner, therefore, pray: Our Father in heaven, Hallowed be Your name." There should be awareness of the following five conditions pertaining to prayer:

1.) *Praying in Jesus' name* – "in My name" – John 14:13 and 14, John 15:16. See also John 16:23–24. The name (Jesus) suggests authority and power.
2.) *Praying according to His will* – "…if we ask anything according to His will, he hears us" (1 John 5:14). Our attitude of mind in prayer should be 'Lord, not my will but yours be done'.
3.) *Abiding in Him* – "If you abide in me and My words abide in you, you will ask what you desire, and it shall be done for you" (John 15:7). It is not possible to pray correctly apart from knowing and believing the teachings of the Lord Jesus Christ.
4.) *Obedience* – "And whatever we ask, we receive from Him, because we keep His commandments, and do those things that are pleasing in His sight" (1 John 3:22). God does hear and answer prayer.
5.) *Forgiveness* – "And whenever you stand praying if you have anything against anyone forgive him, that your Father in heaven may also forgive you your trespasses" (Mark 11:25). Remember, Jesus said "Father, forgive them" while He was on the cross (Luke 23:34). This request for forgiveness was for His persecutors.

The subject of forgiveness is explored further in the chapter on **Forgiveness and the Christian**.

How is your prayer life? We can speak to God in prayer audibly or inaudibly depending on our surroundings and or the occasion. From the Scriptures, different postures in prayer are noted, for example:

Standing – Mark 11:25 – "And when you stand praying," 1 Kings 8:22 – "Solomon stood before the altar of the Lord in the presence of the assembly of Israel."

Kneeling – Luke 22:41 – The Lord knelt to pray in Gethsemane. When Solomon began his prayer (1 Kings 8:22) he was standing. When Solomon finished his prayer, he was kneeling (1 Kings 8:54).

Prostrate – Matthew 26:39 and Mark 14:35 – The Lord Jesus in Gethsemane.

Uplifted eyes – John 11:41 & John 17:1 – Jesus "lifted up His eyes" to God His Father in heaven.

Some Types and Models of Biblical Prayers

Type of Prayer/ Meaning	Old Testament Example	New Testament Example	Jesus' Teaching And Or Example
Praise Adoring God for who He is as well as expressing honour and gratitude to Him	1 Chronicles 29:10–13 – David adoring God – See also Ps 34:1–3; Ps 69:30	Luke 1:46–55 – The Magnificat by the Virgin Mary	Matthew 6:9 & 13b – Note: Matthew 6:9–13 is a model prayer Jesus taught the disciples
Thanksgiving Expressing gratitude to God for what He has done	Psalm 92:1–2; Psalm 105:1–7; 1 Chronicles 16:8	1 Thessalonians 5:16–18; Ephesians 5:20; Philippians 4:6	Luke 17:11–19
Confession Acknowledging sin, helplessness and seeking God's mercy	Psalm 51 – David's confession – note verse 3: "For I acknowledge my transgressions"	Luke 18:13 – The tax collector confesses. "… standing afar off, would not so much as raise his eyes to heaven, but beat his breast saying, 'God, be merciful to me a sinner.'"	Luke 15:11–24; Luke 18:10–14

Forgiveness Seeking mercy for personal sin or the sin of others	Daniel 9:4–19 – Daniel in confession identified himself with the sins of Israel and asked for forgiveness	Acts 7:60 – Stephen asked forgiveness for those who were about to make a martyr of him	Matthew 6:12; Luke 6:27–36
Confidence Affirming God's all-sufficiency and the believer's security in his love	Psalm 23; 2 Chron 14:11 – Asa's prayer; 2 Chron 20:5–12 – Jehoshaphat's prayer	Luke 2:29–32 – Simeon declared that his eyes had seen God's salvation	Matthew 6:5–15; Matthew 7:11
Petition Making personal request to God	Genesis 24:12–14 – Abraham's servant seeking a bride for Isaac	Acts 1:24–26 – When Matthias was chosen as a replacement for Judas	Matthew 7:7–12 – (Ask, seek and knock – verse 7)
Intercession Requesting God on behalf of another	Nehemiah chapter 1 Nehemiah intercedes on behalf of the children of Israel	Philippians 1:9–11 – 1 Timothy 2:1 speaks of "supplications, prayers, intercessions and giving of thanks"	John 17:9; John 17:20–21
Benediction Seeking or announcing God's blessing	Numbers 6:24–26 – The priestly blessing by Aaron and his sons	Romans 15:13; 2 Cor 13:14; Hebrews 13:20–21; Jude 24–25	Luke 24:50–51

We should never give up praying. Rather, we should pray much, pouring out our hearts to our loving heavenly Father who knows all our needs and is able to address them perfectly according to His will. In Luke 18:1-8, Jesus spoke a parable to explain that "men ought always to pray and not lose heart" (Luke 18:1). The parable explains how an unjust judge granted a widow her petition against her adversaries due to her persistence in appearing before him. Jesus said, "And shall not God avenge His own elect who cry out day and night to Him, though He bears long with them? I tell you that He will avenge them speedily" (Luke 18:7-8a). We should pray, we should believe and expect God to answer. He hears our prayers whether we speak audibly or inaudibly.

As we read and study the Bible, meditate on God's word and pray, Christians should always be aware of the old and new natures within them. This is vital in seeking to live a life of heart and soul satisfaction, lasting joy and happiness and maintain Christian growth.

Chapter 9
The Old Nature and the New Nature

"Do not lie to one another, since you have put off the old man
with his deeds, And have put on the new man who is renewed
in knowledge according to the image of Him who created him"
(Colossians 3:9–10).

Every Christian possesses two natures and this must be understood if one is to grow and make spiritual progress. These two natures are called the 'old nature' or the 'old man' and the 'new nature' or the 'new man'.

The old sinful nature was inherited at birth and is incurably bad. The new divine nature is received to do good. Note that the new nature cannot sin because it is born of God (1 John 3:9) and it is a divine nature (2 Peter 1:4). The old nature resides with the Christian person as long as he resides on earth. The new nature stays with him eternally that is beyond his physical death or his translation without dying. During this life, the believer experiences constant conflict between the two natures as both the old and the new are opposed to each other.

The conflict can but need not prevent us from doing the things God wants us to do if we are led by the Holy Spirit (Galatians 5:16–18).

Galatians 5:19–21 mentions 17 'works of the flesh'. It may seem hard for one to avoid them all but there are nine easier things to live out. If one walks in the Spirit then love, joy, peace, longsuffering, gentleness, goodness, faith, meekness, and temperance (Self-control) will be seen in one's life. These characteristics, which are the fruit of the Spirit (Galatians 5:22–23), provide a clear message that a believer is living to please the Lord through the working of the indwelling Holy Spirit.

The fruit of the Spirit should be constantly on display in every believer's life. For instance, your attitude, speech and actions have a lot to do in the glorification of Jesus Christ. The following scriptures are reminders:

- Colossians 4:6 – "Let your speech always be with grace, seasoned with salt, that you may know how you ought to answer each one."
- Ephesians 4:29 – "Let no corrupt word proceed out of your mouth, but what is good for necessary edification, that it may impart grace to the hearers."
- 1 Peter 1:15 – "But as he who called you is holy, you also be holy in all your conduct."

Can others see evidences of the fruit of the Spirit being displayed in your life?

Note the following three tables.

Table 1

The Old Nature is Called	Scriptural References	The New Nature is Called	Scriptural References
The old man	Romans 6:6; Ephesians 4:22; Colossians 3:9	The new man	Ephesians 4:24; Colossians 3:10
The body of sin	Romans 6:6	The inward man	Romans 7:22
The flesh	Romans 8:7–8; Romans 7:18, 23	The mind	Romans 7:25

Table 2

Characteristics of the Old Nature	Scriptural References	Characteristics of the New Nature	Scriptural References
Of the old nature, it is said that it: Is enmity against God	Romans 8:7	Of the new nature, it is said that it: Delights in the law of God	Romans 7:22
Is not subject to the law of God nor can be	Romans 8:7	Minds the things of the Spirit	Romans 8:5
Cannot please God	Romans 8:8	Fulfils the righteousness of the law	Romans 8:4
Minds the things of the flesh	Romans 8:5	Has no condemnation	Romans 8:1
Wars against the new nature	Romans 7:23	Is renewed in knowledge after the image of Him that created him	Colossians 3:10

Table 3

How to deal with the Old Nature	Scriptural References	How to deal with the New Nature	Scriptural References
Mortify its deeds through the Spirit	Romans 8:13 KJV; Colossians 3:5 KJV		
Put it off	Ephesians 4:22; Colossians 3:8–9	Put it on	Ephesians 4:24
Crucify it	Romans 6:6; Galatians 5:24	Walk in it	Galatians 5:16
Reckon it dead	Romans 6:11	Serve in it	Romans 7:6

The devil will always tempt the Christian to function in the old nature instead of the new. At first, Satan will try to get the Christian not to serve God. If this fails, he will try to get the Christian to serve God in the old nature. This means that Satan will try to get the Christian to serve in the energy of the flesh, using fleshly aims, fleshly methods and fleshly strength, instead of using God's strength to do God's work in God's way for His glory.

Work for the Lord done in the flesh has little or no spiritual value. This fleshly work is always hard and barren; there is little sense of fellowship with God. Work done for the Lord with the help of the Holy Spirit, may be hard and challenging but will always carry with it, the sweet sense of love and grace. The Christian experiences peace and rest of soul about it all, knowing that God is always in control no matter what trials and temptations come to him.

Chapter 10
Some Distinguishing Qualities of a Growing Christian

"Since you have purified your souls in obeying the truth through the Spirit in sincere love of the brethren, love one another fervently with a pure heart, having been born again, not of corruptible seed but incorruptible, through the word of God which lives and abides forever" (1 Peter 1:22-23).

"Therefore, laying aside all malice, all deceit, hypocrisy, envy, and all evil speaking, as newborn babes, desire the pure milk of the word, that you may grow thereby, if indeed you have tasted that the Lord is gracious" (1 Peter 2:1-3).

The apostle Peter presents three distinguishing qualities of a growing Christian. Along with each trait, he also adds some more motivating factors that prompt a Christian to live in a certain way. We, therefore, see a mixture of responsibilities and privileges of a Christian. A healthy and growing Christian will: (1) love other Christians, (2) lay aside all evil, and (3) long for the pure milk of the word.

As we know, the Bible teaches that our first love is to God (Mark 12:30; 1 John 4:19; Deuteronomy 6:4–5).

(1) Love other Christians - "Love one another" (1 Peter 1:22).

Observe four things about this love:-

i. *Sincere love*: Unfeigned love – not a show, not just in words, not hypocritical but true.
ii. *Brotherly love*: Love of the brethren with family affection because we are of one family; the Family of God.
iii. *Fervent love*: Loving deeply and passionately showing care and concern.
iv. *Heart-love*: Love from a pure heart. A healthy heart beats spontaneously and blood flows naturally. Similarly, our love should flow instinctively from a healthy heart, from the depths of our innermost being!

What makes love an essential mark of a Christian? Two reasons can be considered. Firstly, our right relationship with the Lord. "Now that you have purified yourselves by obeying the truth so that you have sincere love for your brothers…" (1 Peter 1:22 NIV). What Peter says is this, a believer in Christ heard the gospel, obeyed the truth and is cleansed from his sins and that leads naturally to love for God as well as for man. Obedience to Christ shows love for Him. When a person loves God and maintains a right fellowship with Him, loving the brethren becomes very natural. If we fail to deal with our fellow brethren in divine love we need to examine our own life. The problem may not be with others but with us. If we are not right with God it is very difficult to be right with people. Secondly, our new life. "Having been born again, not of corruptible seed but incorruptible…" (1 Peter 1:23). Another factor that makes love mandatory is our new life.

By virtue of our regeneration by the supernatural work of the Holy Spirit, using the word of God, we have received a new nature. This divine nature will never lie because it has been produced by the imperishable seed; the word of God. It is the indwelling new nature that helps us to do what man in his fallen state can never do, this includes showing God's love for one another (Romans 5:5). So our new relationship with God and the indwelling new nature enable us to love others sincerely and fervently. God has given us love in our hearts in plentiful supply by His Holy Spirit.

In His earthly ministry, Jesus taught about love. Here are two examples:

a) In response to a question from one of the scribes concerning which is the first commandment of all, Jesus included, "And you shall love the Lord your God with all your heart, with all your soul, with all your mind, and with all your strength. This is the first commandment. And the second, like it, is this: You shall love your neighbour as yourself. There is no greater commandment than these" (Mark 12:30–31).

b) The Lord Jesus said to His disciples "A new commandment I give to you, that you love one another; as I have loved you, that you also love one another. By this, all will know that you are My disciples if you have love for one another" (John 13:34–35).

We will explore further the subject of love in another chapter of this book. That chapter is entitled **Love and the Christian**, and for that exercise, the focus will mainly be on 1 Corinthians 13.

(2) Lay aside all evil. (1 Peter 2:1).

One might query what is there to 'lay aside' when they are already 'purified' as recorded in 1 Peter 1:22. It is true God has purified Christians at conversion as they obeyed the truth of the gospel. The effect of that cleansing abides forever. That's why we have been called saints. However, in our day-to-day practical life, we need to avoid all forms of filthiness such as "all malice, all deceit, hypocrisy, envy, and all evil speaking" that would defile us. This truth is best illustrated in John chapter 13. While the Lord Jesus Christ was washing the feet of the apostles, Peter forbade Him. When the Lord says, "If I do not wash you, you have no part with me." Peter asked for a complete cleaning, not just feet! Then the Lord Jesus replied, "He who is bathed needs only to wash his feet, but is completely clean..." (John 13:8–10).

When we were born again we were bathed in the blood of Christ, now we need only a cleansing just like we wash our hands or feet often. If we do not examine ourselves repeatedly and make necessary cleaning-up, our fellowship with the Lord and subsequently our spiritual growth itself will be affected. This in turn will affect our relationship with others. So then, we now remind ourselves of the things to lay aside:

a. Malice: This is an all-inclusive term referring to all kinds of evil. It especially speaks of harbouring evil thoughts against another person including holding a grudge. Secretly hoping that some tragedy may come upon someone, or waiting for an opportunity to 'get even' with someone are examples of a malicious heart. In Mark 6:14–28, and note especially verse 19, we have recorded the story relating to the beheading of John the Baptist. This occurred through the instigation of Herod's wife Herodias because John the Baptist had spoken against the adulterous nature of their marriage. This displeased Herodias who wanted John to be killed. She seized on the earliest opportunity to get this done and indeed, it was duly executed in accordance with her wishes.

Believers should not be involved in malicious practices but should be like little children in the school playground who (From my observation in the past) are willing to 'make up' despite their earlier disagreement (Note 1 Corinthians 14:20)

b. Deceit: Deceit involves lying, promise-breaking or misleading someone, any form of dishonesty, or trickery, hidden agenda in dealings with others. There are instances of deceit recorded in the Bible where the deceivers are questioned about their deceitfulness. For example, Jacob questioned Laban after learning he (Jacob) had married Leah and not Rachel as he had expected (Genesis 29:25); Joshua and the Gibeonites, who pretended to be pilgrims from far away (Joshua 9:22) and Saul questioned his daughter Michal when he found out that she had smuggled David safely away so that he escaped from him (1 Samuel 19:17).

The master of deceit is Satan himself, who seeks to mislead and harm the human race. He is called "a liar and the father of it" (John 8:44). In contrast, God is always open and honest with us and seeks our good. The children of God should be just, open and truthful among themselves and with others. These virtuous qualities portray the children of God as persons of integrity. There is a shortage of integrity in today's world.

c. Hypocrisy: Insincerity, pretence. Sweet talk while meeting face to face but condemning or criticising secretly. Hypocrisy is professing to be what one is not and is generally applied to the religious character. This suggests that a hypocrite is a person whose real self and motives are masked, perhaps even from the individual's own self. No Christian, immature or mature, should live a life of hypocrisy; this is forbidden to the Christian (James 3:17).

d. Envy: From a spiritual perspective, envy is a grudging regard for the advantages seen to be enjoyed by others, a feeling of wanting something that belongs to someone else, not happy to see others prospering. It is one of the most odious and detestable of vices. The policy of one who is steeped in envy is, "I do not have, and he also should not have"! Because of the old nature in every Christian, one cannot always stop envy from beginning but one can stop it from continuing. "A sound heart is life to the body, but envy is rottenness to the bones" (Proverbs 14:30).

e. Evil speaking: May be defined as slander, backbiting or defamation. Effort to show themselves good by projecting someone else as bad, they might spread false reports, rumours, or report truth maliciously. This is character assassination and talebearing. However, when a Christian is slandered such a one should endeavour to patiently bear it even as Christ did (See 1 Peter 2:21–23).

A growing Christian can get rid of all the evils mentioned in 1 Peter 2:1, grow spiritually and show true Christian love for others. If one finds it difficult to love or adjust with others such a person ought to examine his own heart as to whether the new birth has indeed taken place.

(3) Long for the pure milk of the Word (1 Peter 2:2).

Peter compares the word of God to milk, which is a wholesome food, especially for children. As a newborn babe, a Christian should crave spiritual food. Nobody teaches a child to cry for milk! A desire for the word of God is a normal outcome of our new birth. As the absence of an appetite for food is a sign of abnormality, so it is in a Christian's life. If one has no interest whatsoever to read and understand the word of God, this is serious and should be checked out and addressed.

It is good to check our appetite. The sad thing is that we are worried over the loss of appetite in our physical realm but maybe less bothered over the loss of spiritual appetite. The Lord Jesus said to the believing Jews, "If you abide in My word, you are My disciples indeed" (John 8:31). Delight in the law of the Lord is a mark of a righteous man (Psalm 1:2). What do we do when our children lose their appetite? We take them to the doctor's, and sometimes the suggestion is to check if there is any worm creating problems inside the body. That is exactly what we need to do when we lose a desire for the word of God. We need to check ourselves spiritually!

Check on sins that easily ensnare us and mar our spiritual perspective and our aspiration for the things of God. As mentioned previously, we need to thoroughly test our life within and ruthlessly deal with anything that is against the purposes of God. Such a cleansing will inspire us to love, read, obey God's word as well as give us an appetite for it.

What should prompt us to have a desire for God's Word? Tasting is only the beginning (1 Peter 2:3). Other than our aim of growing, the writer adds one thing more that should force us to crave for the word of God. "You have tasted that the Lord is gracious" (1 Peter 2:3). According to Peter, our experience of salvation (Being born again) is only a tasting. There is much more to enjoy in spiritual life. Constant meditation of the Scriptures will help us feed on the Lord Jesus Christ and the more we feed on Him the more will be our desire to know Him and to pray to Him. That in turn will help us to grow in the Lord and enjoy the Christian life.

Growth is a natural consequence where there is life. It is interesting and sometimes exciting to play with a little child and especially to keep track of its physical, intellectual, emotional and social development. However, it is not such an exciting moment when we observe that the child might be lagging behind in one of these areas. In the field of education, it is expected to use resources to assist children to reach their potential. Just as we expect normal growth in proportion to age, every child of God should grow in his spiritual life. The Bible tells us that the Corinthians did not grow spiritually as was expected so they were admonished for their immaturity by the apostle Paul (1 Corinthians 3:1–3). The Hebrew

Christians were also lacking in spiritual progress so the writer of Hebrews admonished them for their failure to grow spiritually (Hebrews 5:12–14). In each case, the writer sought to diagnose the problems and to exhort the church regarding their solution.

It is important for the child of God to be able to discern and tell the difference between correct and incorrect use of the Scriptures. Our capacity to feast on deeper knowledge of God (Solid food) is determined by our spiritual growth and vice versa. As we grow in the Lord and put into practice what we have learned, our capacity to avoid the very appearance of evil will also be enlarged.

Every Christian and especially those with the spiritual gifts of evangelism, pastoring and teaching, must of necessity learn and know from the Bible that there is no private interpretation for any verse or verses of Scripture. God has so graciously revealed His mind to us through His Word. The Holy Spirit opens our understanding and guides us into the truth so "that we should no longer be children, tossed to and fro and carried about with every wind of doctrine, by the trickery of men, in the cunning craftiness of deceitful plotting but speaking the truth in love, may grow up in all things into Him who is the head, Christ" (Ephesians 4:14–15).

A Christian, infant or mature, is marked by sincere love, pure life and a craving for the word of God as well as a healthy prayer life. Such a one has tasted of the goodness of the Lord Jesus Christ and this gives motivation to know Him more. It also motivates him to practise forgiveness as Jesus taught and did, to grow more and more spiritually, and to have victory over sin.

Chapter 11
Adjusting Your Christian Life to God

"I have been crucified with Christ; It is no longer I who live,
but Christ lives in me; and the life which I now live in the flesh
I live by faith in the Son of God, who loved me and gave
Himself for me" (Galatians 2:20).

God has made provision for every Christian to enjoy a life marked by peace, victory and hope. When you become a Christian, you should willingly adjust your life to God's way. God is now your new Master. He owns you and it is perfectly reasonable to do whatever He asks of you considering the enormous sacrifice which Jesus paid to redeem you from Satan and hell (See Romans 12:1–2). You can do this when you surrender your wills to His will. Once you have adjusted your life to Him, that is, His purposes and His ways, you are in a position to serve God according to His will for you. The apostle Paul, in his letter to the Galatian Christians, says, "I have been crucified with Christ; it is no longer I who live but Christ lives in me and the life which I now live in the flesh I live by faith in the Son of God, who loved me and gave Himself for me" (Galatians 2:20).

God-directed adjustments prepare one for obedient service. One cannot please God if one insists on continuing in the same place of abode when God calls and sends. Adjustments and obedience are required. That is true throughout Scripture. For example:

- Noah, "having found grace in the eyes of the Lord" could not continue life as usual and build an ark at the same time (Genesis 6).
- Abram, (Who was later named Abraham – Genesis 17:5) could not stay in Ur or Haran and father a nation in Canaan. He was 75 years old when having heard the call of God, he departed from Haran (Genesis 12:1–8).
- Moses could not stay on the backside of the desert herding sheep, and stand before Pharaoh at the same time. God had called to him from the midst of the burning bush and instructed him to go to Pharaoh (Exodus 3).
- David had to leave his sheep to become king. He was the youngest of Jesse's sons and was chosen by God to replace King Saul (1 Samuel 16:1–13).
- Isaiah, "a man of unclean lips", who dwelt "in the midst of a people of unclean lips" could not be commissioned by God to take the message to the people before his iniquity was taken away and his sin purged (Isaiah 6:1–10).
- Amos had to leave the sycamore trees and sheep breeders in order to preach in Israel (Amos 7:14–15).

- Jonah had to leave his home and overcome self-will in order to preach in Nineveh (Jonah 1:1–3; 3:1–4).
- Peter and Andrew, James and John had to leave their fishing businesses in order to follow Jesus (Matthew 4:18–22).
- Matthew had to leave his tax collector's booth to follow Jesus (Matthew 9:9).
- Saul of Tarsus (Later called Paul) had to completely change direction in his life in order to be used by God to preach the gospel to the Gentiles (Acts 9:1–19).
- When my wife Nurkle and I were called to the mission field in Jamaica, we were both occupied in our secular jobs in the field of education in London, United Kingdom (UK). I worked then as a Headmaster of a Primary School and as an Office for Standards in Education (OFSTED) Team Inspector. My wife worked as Principal Admissions Officer and Schools Exclusions Coordinator for a Local Education Authority. We were available to Him and:

- Went where He wanted us to go.
- Became what He wanted us to be.
- Did what he wanted us to do.

You will observe from the above examples that individuals had to adjust their lives and circumstances in response to God's specific calls and assignments. Regardless of how occupied they were previously, they were available to Him. Perhaps He has some special assignment for you. Are you prepared to say yes Lord, I am available, Your will be done?

Lord, Not My Will

1) *Lord, not my will but Your will must be done*
   You have chosen me, You have willed for me
   That which is best comes only from You
   My Lord and my Saviour, Your will must be done.

2) *No other path, but the path which You choose*
   Other paths though bright and attractive be
   The narrow path is pleasing to You
   My Lord and my Saviour, that path must I tread.

3) *No other work but the work which You give*
   In the things I do, I should honour You
   Work for the Lord while now it is day
   My Lord and my Saviour, your work must be done.
   (© Copyright 1983 by Winston G Litchmore)

Chapter 12
Love and the Christian

***"Though I speak with the tongues of men and of angels, but
have not love, I have become sounding brass or a clanging
cymbal" (1 Corinthians 13:1).***

It is wonderful to love and be loved and to see this in evidence especially among the people of God. Jesus said to His disciples, "A new commandment I give unto you, that ye love one another. By this shall all men know that ye are my disciples if ye have love one to another" (John 13 34–35 KJV). Love is to be exercised towards one another, not only because we belong to the same earthly nation, colour, group or class but firstly because we belong to Christ. The love between saints in Christ is to be the expression of the peerless, incomparable, love of the Lord Jesus Christ Himself.

True love is from God – it does not exist apart from Him. We know that God is One in Three Persons.

- It is difficult to think of God the Father without thinking of love – God is love.
- It is difficult to think of the Lord Jesus Christ without thinking of love.
- It is difficult to think of the Holy Spirit without thinking of love.

Head knowledge should not be separated from practical living. You cannot have a correct understanding of God without wanting to live in a way that pleases God. You must walk the talk!

Love in Evidence

It is expected that every child of God should demonstrate love in his life. Live a Life proved by love. Why? Because as Christians, "We know that we have passed from death unto life because we love the brethren. He who does not love his brother abides in death" (1 John 3:14).

i. We know that we live because we love.
ii. "We love the brethren". This means we love our brothers and sisters in Christ.
iii. We love them for Christ's sake.
iv. We love them for the truth's sake
v. We love them for their own sake.
vi. We love them when the world hates them.
vii. We love their company, their good examples, and their exhortations.

   viii. We love them despite the drawbacks of infirmity, old age, low self-esteem, unemployment, good or bad living conditions, et cetera.
   ix. We love them when they do us wrong and do not return our love.

There is a popular idea today which seems to be that if we love God enough, we will eventually love our brothers and sisters in Christ. We learn from the Scriptures that if there is any brother or any sister, who does not love actively, operationally, then his or her relationship with God is seriously wrong. There are many excuses and watered-down phrases for not loving people.

- "Oh, I love him in the Lord but I don't like his mannerisms.
- Zipporah is all right but she is so hard to get to know.
- Rusticle has emotional problems.
- Alphonia comes from such a difficult background."

In the sight of God, it is all hypocrisy. God never said in the Bible, that you are to love your brother if he is a keen Christian, well dressed, a good evangelist, and if he gets on with you. No! In fact, the Lord Jesus Christ tells us in the Sermon on the Mount to love our enemies! He indicates that real love does not begin until we love our enemies.

Jesus also teaches us that we should love our neighbour as ourselves.

- Our love-filled, Spirit-filled lives should motivate us towards soul winning.
- We love our enemies and our neighbours.
- We pray for opportunities to witness to them.
- Making and taking opportunities to witness to them – we become real soul winners.

The supreme example of love is found at Calvary's Cross, where the holy, sinless Son of God died for a world of rebellious, defiant sinners. The Apostle Paul showed his willingness to love consistently when he wrote to the Corinthians, "I will very gladly spend and be spent for you; though the more abundantly I love you, the less I be loved" (2 Corinthians 12:15).

Love and Spiritual Gifts

In 1 Corinthians 12, the Apostle Paul gave evidence of the Corinthian Christians' need to portray love whenever they exercise spiritual gifts. Chapter 13 defines real love, and Chapter 14 shows how love works. Love is most important when exercising spiritual gifts.

Spiritual Gifts

In the Old Testament, God gave certain people the ability to serve Him in special ways. God filled Bezalel "with the Spirit of God, with skill, ability, and knowledge in all kinds of crafts" to shape articles for the tabernacle (Exodus 31:3). See also Exodus 31:6, Judges 3:10, 14:6. When we speak of spiritual gifts, we mean abilities given to believers by the Holy Spirit (1 Corinthians 12:7).

Four New Testament passages deal specifically with spiritual gifts **(Romans 12, 1 Corinthians 12, Ephesians 4, and 1 Peter 4:10)**. ***Three of them place gifts squarely in the context of ministry within the Body of Christ.*** These passages teach that each believer has a gift or gifts, that is, a special capacity to contribute to the well-being and growth of other believers. Spiritual gifts are to be used to build up other Christians, create unity, express love and reach new believers (Ephesians 4:11–13).

There are different gifts that God has distributed sovereignly within the Body (1 Corinthians 12:6–7). When Christians live together in love, actively seeking to serve and help one another, these gifts are exercised and the whole Body is strengthened. Thus, Peter says, "Each one should use whatever gift he has received to serve others, faithfully administering God's grace in its various forms" (1 Peter 4:10). God's grace is evidenced tangibly in the Body through the gifts of the Holy Spirit.

It is important to note that each New Testament passage on spiritual gifts focuses our attention on the Christian community. Gifts are best exercised within the context of a caring, loving fellowship. Although individuals have different gifts, love is available to all. "…the love of God has been poured out in our hearts by the Holy Spirit who was given to us" (Romans 5:5). The priority is to get to know the Lord more closely and to get to know His voice clearly. As we have sustained fellowship with our Lord through prayer and meditation of God's Word, we will discover the spiritual gifts with which He has endowed us. As we get to know Him more and more, we love Him more and more and are delighted and excited to serve Him, the King of kings and Lord of all lords. Serving the Lord carries its challenges and persecutions but it should be a joy to serve the Lord as we appreciate the enormous sacrifice that Jesus made in order to pay for our sins, past, present and future as I mentioned earlier in this book.

Love in 1 Corinthians 13

1 Corinthians 13, the 'love chapter', can easily be sectioned into four parts, which can be summarised as:

(1) Verses 1–3: These gifts: tongues, prophecy, faith and giving, are ineffective unless they are lovingly exercised to benefit others. Even their most spectacular manifestations mean nothing unless motivated by love.
(2) Verses 4–7: These qualities will characterize those who exercise their gifts in love. Indeed they are the thoughts and actions of love.
(3) Verses 8–12: In these verses, we note the permanence of love contrasted with the temporary character of gifts.
(4) Verse 13: We see the superiority of love over the virtues of faith and hope. Faith is the foundation and content of God's message, Hope is the attitude and focus, Love is the action. Of faith, hope and love, love is the greatest.

The apostle Paul uses the Greek word *agape*. The ancient Greeks had four different words, eros, storge, philia, agape, we translate as love. It is important to understand the difference between the words and why Paul chose the Greek word agape here.

i. Eros is one word for love. It describes erotic love. This refers to sexual love. This love does not necessarily have at heart the highest welfare of those participating.
ii. Storge is the second word for love. It refers to family love; the kind of love there is between parent and child or between family members in general.
iii. Philia is the third word for love. It speaks of a brotherly friendship and affection. It might be described as the highest love of which man, without God's help, is capable.
iv. Agape is the fourth word for love. It is a love that loves without changing. It is a self-giving love that gives without demanding or expecting repayment. This is love so great that it can be given to the unlovable or unappealing. This is love that loves even when it is rejected. Agape love gives, and loves because it wants to. It gives because it loves; it does not love in order to receive. This love hates the wrongdoing but loves the one who does the wrongdoing. It desires one's highest good and gives needed support.

It is worth remembering that:

a) The greatest love is God's love. "God is love" (1 John 4:8, 16). God's gift of love to the world is His Son Jesus Christ (John 3:16).
b) "…the love of God has been poured out in our

hearts by the Holy Spirit who was given to us" (Romans 5:5).
c) Agape love seeks one's highest good at all times and in all circumstances.

We should endeavour to apply the following behaviours of love, based upon 1 Corinthians 13:4–7, in our relationships and responses to others. Love:

- Suffers long – It is 'long-minded', slow to take offence [Holy relationships].
- Is kind – It is disposed to be useful to others; good-natured and wishes others well [Holy purposes].
- Does not envy – No one or anything is begrudged or bad feelings created over another's prosperity [Holy heart].
- Does not parade itself – 'Bragging rights' are never claimed. It does not seek or want admiration or applause [Holy speech].
- Is not puffed up – There is no display of arrogance or attitude of a mind swelled with its own importance [Holy service].
- Does not behave rudely – It is neither rude nor crude and it does not act unbecomingly [Holy behaviour].
- Does not seek its own – Not selfish or self-centred and it does nothing for personal interest [Holy desires].
- Is not easily provoked – It is not irritable, easily angered or quick-tempered [Holy temperament].
- Thinks no evil – It does not take into account a

wrong and it does not keep track of evil, therefore, it keeps no record of wrongdoing [Holy bookkeeping].
- Does not rejoice in iniquity – It is not glad over evil and never finds reason to be vindictive, hence there is no rejoicing in unrighteousness [Holy conscience].
- Rejoices in the truth – It becomes involved in spreading the gospel and gets excited about good [Holy mind].
- Bears all things – It always seeks to protect, based on truth even if misunderstood [Holy stability].
- Believes all things – It tries to put things in the best light possible; it is not superstitious [Holy values].
- Hopes all things – It lives, looking for the 'silver lining' and always trusts things will work out well for the best [Holy expectations].
- Endures all things – It perseveres and is steadfast and immovable against all odds [Holy sacrifice].

Christians are challenged to watch for opportunities God may bring across our lives in order for us to love more perfectly. It is to the good that we check ourselves often and ask God to help us evaluate our 'love-life' based on the perfect standard of His beloved Son, our Lord Jesus Christ. Each believer should watch for specific ways in which God may be guiding him towards showing love to others and doing so with joy.

1 Corinthians 13:4–8 **What Love Does**	1 Corinthians 13:4–6 **What Love Does Not**
Suffers long (Verse 4)	Does not envy (Verse 4)
Is kind (Verse 4)	Does not parade itself (Verse 4)
Rejoices in truth (Verse 6)	Is not puffed up (Verse 4)
Bears all things (Verse 7)	Does not behave rudely (Verse 5)
Believes all things (Verse 7)	Does not seek its own (Verse 5)
Hopes all things (Verse 7)	Is not provoked (Verse 5)
Endures all things (Verse 7)	Thinks no evil (Verse 5)
Never fails (Verse 8)	Does not rejoice in iniquity (Verse 6)

Chapter 13
Forgiveness and the Christian

"And be kind one to another, tender-hearted, forgiving one another, even as God in Christ forgave you"
(Ephesians 4:32).

The word forgiveness means the action of forgiving or the process of being forgiven. To forgive is to give someone a release from the wrong that he has done to you, stop feeling angry or resentful towards the individual for an offence or mistake, cancel the debt, release the person from the charges, give up any right of retaliation and sticking to that non-retaliation commitment.

From a Biblical perspective, God's forgiveness is the cancelling by God of the sinner's debt and guilt on the basis of Christ's death for sinners. The conditions are repentance and faith in Jesus Christ ("In Him we have redemption through His blood, the forgiveness of sins, according to the riches of His grace" – Ephesians 1:7).

In His ministry, our Lord Jesus Christ taught and demonstrated that the subject of forgiveness is very important in our lives. He practised what He taught, for example, while on the cross and placed between two criminals He said, "Father forgive them, for they do not know what they do" (Luke 23:34). This prayer was being offered for the crowd who were present and by extension all humankind.

Remember, sins which were committed before an individual became a Christian will never be held against that individual again by God. No charge can be brought against the believer, for God has justified, declared righteous, those whose sins Christ has taken away. "Who shall bring a charge against God's elect? It is God who justifies. Who is he who condemns? It is Christ who died, and furthermore is also risen, who is even at the right hand of God, who also makes intercession for us" (Romans 8:33–34).

One of the many teachings on the subject of forgiveness is found in the prayer Jesus taught His disciples. "And forgive us our debts, as we forgive our debtors" (Matthew 6:12), paraphrased, "and forgive us our sins, just as we have forgiven those who have sinned against us" (TLB).

If you want to be forgiven then you must forgive others. An unforgiving spirit is contrary to God's will and practice and could result in some of the following:

- Fellowship with God our heavenly Father is interrupted.
- The devil potentially gains an entrance through our unwillingness to forgive. This can be manifested by unrighteous anger which one refuses to relinquish (Ephesians 4:26–27).
- Prayers will be hindered and will not be answered (See Psalm 66:18).
- The Holy Spirit is grieved because spiritual progress is interrupted (See Ephesians 4:30–32).
- We waste time (And emotional energy) nursing a wounded spirit instead of cultivating a Christ like spirit.
- We lose the blessing of God in our life and ministry.
- We become like those we refuse to forgive because we sin against God when we do so.

It is believed that unforgiveness is the number one problem with many Christians and among many a Christian group and must be dealt with severely.

How do I know when I have truly forgiven my debtors or trespassers?

I know I have forgiven my debtors or trespassers when I:

i. Face what they did and forgive them anyway – God's Word says I should! "And forgive us our debts, as we forgive our debtors" (Matthew 6:12).
ii. Do not keep bringing the matter up to my former debtors and I do not talk about it to others.
iii. Show mercy instead of judgement (Matthew 5:7 and James 2:13).
iv. Refuse to speak evil of the wrongdoer or wrongdoers and choose not to dwell on their wrongdoing (Ephesians 4:31–32).
v. Ask God to bless them and enable me to help them when I can and not to rejoice at their calamities (Romans 12:14–20).
vi. Am patient and kind to those who find it hard and take long to deal with emotional pain and upset.

As we consider further the subject of forgiveness, we note **Three Biblical Calls to Forgiveness**: (1) Forgive to restore a sinning brother – Matthew 18:15–17. (2) Forgive so that your prayers are not hindered – Mark 11:25–26. (3) Forgive so that you do not grieve the Holy Spirit – Ephesians 4:30–32.

(1) Forgive to restore a sinning brother – Matthew 18:15–17

i. It is a simple straightforward plan to forgive your brother who has sinned against you.

a. You go to him alone, not telling anyone else.
b. You go immediately, praying for reconciliation (<u>reconciliation</u> = the end of a disagreement and the return to friendly relations; restored relationship – 2 Corinthians 5:18–20).

ii. You lovingly tell your brother your assessment of the problem between you both. You should seek to forgive soonest. However, he needs to be told about the wrong. The wrong must be factual and truthful and based on the revealed will of God in His Word.
iii. If your brother responds, you forgive him and you are both reconciled.
iv. If he does not respond, you take another step, involve others.
v. If that does not resolve the problem, you go to the church in an effort to gain your brother, to effect reconciliation.

If you are that sinning brother as mentioned above, then you need to heed the word of God from Romans 12:18, where the apostle Paul addresses the subject of the believers living out the gospel. It states that "If it be possible, as much as depends on you, live peaceably with all men." One segment of the fruit of the Holy Spirit is 'peace'. The believer should love peace and seek to be at peace with all men. You should therefore urgently and increasingly pursue peace. The Holy Spirit who knows the heart leads us into repentance, confession and restoration as we pray and exercise faith in God's word.

Note well: (a) Christ's death provided for the removal of the barrier of sin to bring people back into a right relationship with God. (b) In addition to reconciling us to Himself, God has given us the ministry of reconciliation. How do we fulfil this ministry of reconciliation? Follow the teaching, the teaching which Jesus taught His disciples (Matthew 18:15–17) and the teaching of other Scriptures previously mentioned in this book. Forgiveness is one of the most powerful tools which the Lord Jesus has given to us as we interact with other humankind in marriages, in family life, church settings, community life and workplace. It is a good thing if all believers ask the Lord for the enabling to be effective peacemakers whether we are involved in a quarrel or are on the outside looking in.

Forgiveness should be unlimited. Ponder Matthew 18:21–22: "Then Peter came to Him and said, Lord, how often shall my brother sin against me, and I forgive him? Up to seven times?" Jesus said to him, "I do not say to you, up to seven times, but up to seventy times seven." The rabbis taught that people should forgive those who offend them but only three times. Peter trying to be especially generous, asked Jesus, if seven times were enough to forgive someone. Jesus answered, "seventy times seven." This means that we should not keep a record of how many times we forgive someone. We should always forgive those who are truly repentant, no matter how many times they trespass against us and ask us to forgive them. Christ forgave us of our indebtedness to Him and loves us dearly and deeply despite our sin. We should forgive others and be willing to do so at the greatest sacrifice to ourselves and even to our good reputation.

(2) Forgive so that your prayers are not hindered

Jesus taught: "And whenever you stand praying if you have anything against anyone, forgive him that your heavenly Father may also forgive you your trespasses" (Mark 11:25). Effective prayer is vital to any Christian as well as to any church. The first meeting of the early church was a prayer meeting (Acts 1:14 and 24). When believers agree in prayer, good things happen.

We cannot pray effectively unless we forgive. The Christian who is obedient to the word of God regarding forgiveness will agree with this positive declaration from the Epistle of John, "And whatever we ask we receive from Him because we keep His commandments and do those things that are pleasing in His sight" (1 John 3:22). When Jesus taught His disciples to pray, He made forgiveness the cornerstone of their relationship with God.

- God has forgiven our sins; we must now forgive those who have wronged us.
- To remain unforgiving shows we have not understood that we ourselves deeply need to be forgiven.

- Think of some persons who have wronged you. Have you forgiven them?
- How will God deal with you if He treats you as you treat others?

(3) Forgive so that you do not grieve the Holy Spirit

Why did the early church have such great power? The believers were weak and imperfect people but the Holy Spirit was the source of their power. They were filled with the Holy Spirit. The Holy Spirit does not leave the believer even when he is holding a malice because once He lives in his heart He abides there forever (Ephesians 4:30). When we do not forgive, we grieve the Holy Spirit because instead of being filled with Him we are harbouring malice and anger. Spirit-filled people are not in bondage to malice and anger.

Remember, we should forgive because we have been forgiven. "And be kind to one another, tender-hearted, forgiving one another, even as God in Christ forgave you" (Ephesians 4:32). Since the Holy Spirit lives in us continually we should allow Him access to all areas of our lives and submit to His guidance and counsel. Using the word of God, He produces in us the fruit of the Spirit whose segments are love, joy, peace, longsuffering, kindness, goodness, faithfulness, gentleness and self-control which are to motivate us and set us free to forgive.

Self-assessment questions on forgiveness

- Am I up to date on my forgiving?
- Can I think of someone I need to forgive?
- Am I holding a grudge against anyone?
- What happens to my fellowship with God when I hold a grudge?
- Do I harbour any bitterness against any person?
- Am I talking too much about what others have done to me?
- Am I gathering support against them to defame them?
- Have I forgiven those closest to me who have hurt me so deeply that it caused embarrassment and distress?

If it seems I cannot forgive or if I refuse to forgive, I must remember how much I have been forgiven and therefore ask the Lord to help me to forgive others. My prayer should be: "Lord, I want to be an imitator of Your perfect example." When God forgave me of my sins, I felt a burden had rolled away from me. Similarly, when I forgive others, I relieve them of the burden of guilt, and it also sets me free from the negative effect on myself of the sin committed. I can go further and ask the Lord to erase the sin committed against me from the perpetrator's account. This is forgiveness indeed! Furthermore, it is possible that the one whom I have forgiven is finding it difficult to forgive himself of the wrong. My genuine and earnest prayer, and wise personal interaction bathed in love and magnified in grace, can be most effective here.

In some instances, both parties have wronged each other although one of them started the problem. Both need to acknowledge their own individual fault, apologise and reconcile. If this is done promptly, then the case has been won all around. It should be noted that offence may occur due to ignorance, misunderstanding, wrong assumptions, misinformation, prejudice, personality clash, sickness and other disablements on the part of the offender. The same may be true on the part of the one offended. Whatever the background story, they should 'walk' together through the process of forgiveness and reconciliation, and undertake any practical redress necessary so that they may with one mind and mouth glorify the God and Father of our Lord Jesus Christ (Romans 15:6). In so doing, they maintain the unity and dignity of their Church family and show the world that they are forgiven and forgiving persons. They are Christians and the Holy Spirit feels at home in their hearts which are free from malice, anger and wrath.

A firm and compelling ground for giving and receiving forgiveness is the fact that God, for Christ's sake has forgiven us of an enormous debt of sin which we ourselves could never pay.

Chapter 14
Temptation and the Christian

"No temptation has overtaken you except such as is common to
man; but God is faithful, who will not allow you to be tempted
beyond what you are able, but with the temptation will also
make the way of escape, that you may be able to bear it"
(1 Corinthians 10:13).

The believer has been reading and studying the Bible, meditating on God's Word and praying. He is always aware of his old and new natures and is therefore growing spiritually and having various experiences of the Christian life especially the joy and happiness of sins forgiven. However, every Christian must experience temptation. It is a fact of life while we remain in our present bodies and Satan is at large. We will now explore this subject of Temptation and the Christian.

From the spiritual perspective, temptation is:

(a) To induce or entice a person to sin – (James 1:13–15), "God cannot be tempted by evil, nor does He Himself tempt anyone".
(b) To arouse desire in, to attract – (James 1:13–15).

In this second sense, temptations are inner pressures caused by the interaction of circumstances and the limitations inherent in our humanity. But temptations are also opportunities. When we feel attracted towards doing wrong, we have the opportunity to choose what is right and so to be strengthened spiritually.

Four biblical passages help us to understand temptation. Two of the passages treat temptation as an enticement to sin and two of these passages treat situational temptations in which pressures are created by our humanity itself.

(1) Eve's temptation – (Genesis 3). The passage shows Satan's strategies for weakening human defences. The result: Adam and Eve introduced sin into the human race by yielding to the temptation.

(2) Jesus' temptation – (Matthew 4:1–11, Luke 4:1–13). Satan tries three times to incite Jesus to sin. Jesus who is intrinsically holy cannot sin nor be incited by temptation. James 1:13 states that "God cannot be tempted by evil." The devil quoted Scripture incorrectly; Jesus resisted the temptation by quoting Scriptures correctly. Note what the devil says to Jesus in Luke 4:6–7, "All this authority will I give You, and their glory, for this has been delivered to me, and I give it to whomsoever I wish. Therefore, if You will worship before me, all will be Yours."

It is not possible for Satan to give authority to the Lord Jesus. The Lord Jesus has "authority over all flesh" (John 17:2). The Lord Jesus also declares to His disciples in Matthew 28 that He has authority in heaven and on earth when He says, "All authority has been given to Me in heaven and on earth" (Matthew 28:18). God allows the devil to have authority but only in a measure and only for a period of time, and this is always under God's control. The story of Job is a very interesting example (Job 1:12 and Job 2:6).

(3) Jesus is able to help – (Hebrews 2:14–18). This passage emphasizes Jesus' flesh-and-blood human form, telling us that He experienced temptations like us. Though "He Himself has suffered being tempted," He could not surrender to temptation (Hebrews 5:7–10), because He is God and cannot sin.

(4) Does God tempt? – (James 1:13–15). No, James says, God does not tempt us. We need to understand that God will not tempt us; He tests us as stated previously. The sin of Adam and Eve brought death. It is wonderful to know that the Lord Jesus endured temptation; Jesus passed the test and so can we by His help! Jesus was always filled with the Holy Spirit who led Him into the wilderness for the temptation (Matthew 4:1). Jesus, the Holy One, was always obedient to the will of God His Father but could not, and cannot act on what the devil proposes that He should do.

We notice that in the temptation of Jesus not only did the devil speak but he showed. We see the use of the eyes technique being employed here. Many had fallen to his wiles before just by looking. For example:

Eve: "So when the women saw that the tree was good for food (Lust of the flesh), that it was pleasant to the eyes (Lust of the eyes), and a tree desirable to make one wise (The pride of life), she took of its fruit and ate. She also gave to her husband with her, and he ate" (Genesis 3:6). Adam and Eve had to decide whether God or the devil was speaking the truth. They decided to believe the devil and in doing so they disobeyed God's command. They both sinned! They yielded to temptation rather than resisting it and brought in sin upon all their descendants which includes us.

David: David, a man after God's own heart was tempted, via his eyes. He yielded and committed adultery with Bathsheba. When Saul was chasing David and David had the opportunity of killing him and becoming king, David did not yield to that temptation. But he did not similarly display this resistance in his encounter with Bathsheba because he allowed 'eye-gate' to lead him along the wrong path. David was in the wrong place at the wrong time; he should have been on the battlefield, instead, he stayed in Jerusalem and was drawn by his lust for the flesh. Read 2 Samuel chapter 11 and carefully note verses 1 and 2.

We should be on our guard at all times. The apostle Peter in his epistle writes these words: "Be sober, be vigilant because your adversary, the devil, walks about like a roaring lion, seeking whom he may devour" (1Peter 5:8). Peter was inspired to pen those words, no doubt, through personal experience. In fact, the Lord forewarned Peter about Satan's wiles, "And the Lord said, Simon, Simon! Indeed, Satan has asked for you, that he may sift you as wheat. But I have prayed for you, that your faith should not fail; and when you have returned to Me, strengthen your brethren" (Luke 22:31–32).

Note carefully that Peter later genuinely repented and was mightily used of the Lord in his apostleship, and in the writing of two epistles. In 1 Peter 4:12, he encouraged those who were under persecution and trials. They should conduct themselves patiently and courageously because by so doing they will experience exceeding joy when Christ returns.

Often when we fall or yield to temptation, we try to make excuses or blame someone else. "Let no one say when he is tempted, "I am tempted of God"; for God cannot be tempted by evil, nor does He Himself tempt anyone. But each one is tempted when he is drawn away by his own desires and enticed. Then when desire has conceived, it gives birth to sin and sin, when it is full-grown, brings forth death. Do not be deceived, my beloved brethren" (James 1:13–16). Note well: God does allow us to be tempted or tested but that test is for His Glory, and our own good. What good? It is a means of strengthening our faith. God also provides the resources necessary for one to overcome and be victorious.

Here is comfort for us: "No temptation has overtaken you except such as is common to man but God is faithful, who will not allow you to be tempted beyond what you are able but will with the temptation also make a way to escape, that you may be able to bear it" (1 Corinthians 10:13). The model prayer in Matthew 6:9–13 including Jesus' teaching on the subject of prayer acknowledges that there is a possibility that we fall under temptation. This is an evil from which the prayer asks that we be delivered.

It is important for one to understand that temptation is not sin. From Genesis chapter 3, we learn that the devil introduced the temptation but that it was Adam and Eve who introduced sin on the earth by submitting to the devil's ploy. Christ, who came to earth in a body, was tempted as we are yet remain sinless. Jesus remained sinless because as a member of the Godhead, He cannot sin and will never sin. God the Father, God the Son and God the Holy Spirit, are one God and are absolutely holy.

Throughout His life on earth, Jesus proved that He is God. He was not born of the seed of humankind but was conceived of the Holy Spirit in Mary's virgin womb. It must always be remembered that as God, Jesus is eternal and existed before He was conceived in Mary's womb. His name is Immanuel meaning "God with us" (Isaiah 7:4, Matthew 1:23). Jesus' perfect life and teaching here on earth provide us with clarity on the impeccable nature of God. In His handling of the temptations in the wilderness, Jesus has left us a pattern regarding how we should handle our own temptations.

He "was in all points tempted like as we are, yet without sin" (Hebrews 4:15). Jesus resisted the devil and all his temptations. Luke's gospel tells us that the devil departed from the Lord for a season. "And when the devil had ended all the temptation, he departed from him for a season" (Luke 4:13 KJV).

The devil will not cease tempting or putting the Christian to the test until the Lord's second coming in the clouds, or if He calls for us in death before that event. Until such time, believers should keep their eyes fixed on the Lord Jesus Christ. We must watch and pray lest we enter into temptation. We must resist Satan and resist him in the name of the Lord Jesus Christ by the help of the Holy Spirit, always rightly applying the word of God.

The Christian should always be ready and willing to stand firm against the devil and his tricks. One must "Resist him steadfast in the faith, knowing that the same sufferings are experienced by your brotherhood in the world" (1 Peter 5:9). "Therefore, submit to God. Resist the devil and he will flee from you" (James 4:7). How do we resist the devil? We occupy our hearts and minds with the Lord, feed on God's Word, meditate on it and obey it, live it out in our Christian life. The Christian must have faith and confidence in God's Word; "For whatever is born of God overcomes the world. And this is the victory that has overcome the world, our faith" (1 John 5:4).

The believer is not able to overcome temptations by his own efforts. With the pull of the world and its wicked devices, and the other challenging experiences of life, our own efforts are bound to fail. The Lord Jesus Christ is the one who is always in control of all things and of our lives. Since He is the mighty Conqueror over all our foes, both for now and in the future, we must place our faith in Him at all times. Develop a faith habit on a daily basis. The Lord never fails to succour us and we need Him constantly. Faith in God is the shield that enables us to quench all the fiery darts of the wicked one (Ephesians 6:16).

It must be in our consciousness that the pull toward sin that we experience when tempted comes from our fallen human nature but if we be on our guard and get to know God more and more, we will grow rooted and grounded in the Lord Jesus Christ. Be aware of the subtlety of Satan and of his evil devices. The apostle Paul wrote to the Corinthian Church regarding a situation where they had forgiven and restored a fallen brother saying, "Lest Satan should take advantage of us; for we are not ignorant of his devices" (2 Corinthians 2:11).

Chapter 15
Joy and the Christian

When we speak of joy, we are not speaking of a light-hearted, froth and bubble emotion but of deep-seated contentment and satisfaction in God Himself. In the Bible, that is, both in the Old and New Testaments, joy is consistent with the characteristics both individually of the Christian and corporately of the Church. It is a distinctive characteristic (Quality) of the Christian's life which begins here on earth and continues during eternity. It is not simply an emotion. It is found in God Himself and definitely derived from Him. See Psalm 16:11, Romans 15:13, Philippians 4:4.

Certainly, joy is one of the 'segments' of the fruit of the Spirit and it is deemed functional in the life of the Christian. NOTE: "But the fruit of the Spirit is love, joy, peace, longsuffering, kindness, goodness, faithfulness, gentleness, self-control. Against such there is no law" (Galatians 5:22–23).

Joy is one of the evidences on the display of a Holy Spirit-filled life.

- Joy is delightful - our soul's season of rejoicing has come when joy enters.
- It is demonstrative - it is more than peace; it sparkles, shines, and sings.
- It is stimulating and urges its possessor to undertake brave deeds.
- It is influential for good. Sinners are attracted to the Lord Jesus Christ by the joy of saints.
- It is contagious - others are made glad by our rejoicing.

If you are a Christian, is your life radiating joy to others?

The apostle Paul exhorts the Philippians to "Rejoice in the Lord always. And again I say, rejoice!" (Philippians 4:4). The epistle to the Philippians is peculiarly joyous. The apostle is joyful throughout, and we note:

1) He sweetens prayer with joy (1:4).
2) He rejoices that Christ is preached (1:18).
3) To see the members like-minded with his joy (2:2).
4) It was his joy that he should not run in vain (2:16).
5) His farewell to them was, "Rejoice in the Lord" (3:1).
6) He speaks of those who rejoice in Christ Jesus (3:3)
7) He calls those converted through his preaching, his joy and his crown (4:1).
8) He expresses his joy in their kindness (4:10).

We can learn from the Lord Jesus Christ, who the Bible describes as "A Man of Sorrows and acquainted with grief" (Isaiah 53:3). Despite the truth of the description, we learn that in every moment of His life, there was a true joy. His joy was both present and future. Regarding the present, Jesus could say, "My food is to do the will of Him who sent me and to finish His work" (John 4:34). As to the future, it is written of the Lord Jesus: "Who for the joy that was set before Him endured the cross, despising the shame, and has sat down at the right hand of the throne of God" (Hebrews 12:2).

The world offers "passing pleasures of sin" (Hebrews 11:25) but the Lord Jesus Christ offers lasting joy through the forgiveness of sins. Jesus says: "These things I have spoken to you, that My joy may remain in you, and that your joy may be full" (John 15:11).

- Pleasure is dependent on circumstances but joy is inward and is not disturbed by one's environment.
- Joy is constant but pleasure is always changing.
- True joy is grounded in Jesus Christ, who "is the same yesterday, today, and forever" (Hebrews 13:8).
- Joy is a gift we receive from God. Joy is based on self-sacrifice and pleasure is sometimes based on self-seeking.
- Joy is based on the sacrificial giving of ourselves.

As we ponder the above, we should pay attention to the words Jesus said to His disciples as He encouraged them: "Therefore, you now have sorrow; but I will see you again and your heart will rejoice, and your joy no one will take from you" (John 16:22). And sure enough, the Lord Jesus Christ came to see the disciples in the evening of the day of His resurrection, and they rejoiced at His presence, "Then the disciples were glad when they saw the Lord" (John 20:20).

Peter in his epistle, thinking about the present suffering of the Christians and the return of the Lord Jesus Christ writes, "Whom having not seen you love. Though now you do not see Him, yet believing, you rejoice with joy inexpressible and full of glory" (1 Peter 1:8). Christians who love the Lord Jesus Christ and are following Him in earnest, they joyfully anticipate His return and their being with Him forever. Are you looking forward to seeing the Lord Jesus Christ and being with Him forever? If you are, this should bring you heart and soul satisfaction.

Chapter 16
Concluding Chapter

The concluding chapter of this book serves to remind the reader of its contents, as the author comments briefly on the chapters that have gone before.

Chapter 1. Who Is a Christian?
Being a Christian is not simply about keeping rules and regulations, performing rituals or going to church. A Christian is one who has come to an understanding of the seriousness of being an enemy of God, and has asked for and obtained forgiveness of sins and has received a new spiritual life. Those of us who know that our sins have been forgiven have peace and joy in our hearts although we have challenges in this life.

Chapter 2. Assurance of One's Salvation
To be assured of one's salvation is not by feeling but by knowing through the witness of God's indwelling Holy Spirit. The Holy Spirit gives full confidence that because one has believed in the Lord Jesus Christ and has called upon Him in faith, one has everlasting life and shall not come into condemnation but is passed from spiritual death unto spiritual life. Thus a Christian is assured that he will never go to hell.

Chapter 3. Baptism

One is baptised on the confession of one's faith in Jesus Christ as Saviour and Lord of one's life. The biblical practice is that the individual understands that he is first a Christian and then baptism follows. Baptism involves total immersion under water and rising up out of the water to walk in the newness of life before God and the world.

Chapter 4. Christian Fellowship

It is said that one live coal cannot keep a fire glowing; it needs other pieces with it. The individual Christian needs friendship and support of other Christians. The Christian needs to worship, socialize, study the word of God and grow with a local company of believers. He needs to experience the privileges and responsibilities of that company and come under its disciplines.

Chapter 5. Separation

Separation means more than just 'dividing the men from the boys' or 'the women from the girls'. The apostle Paul writing under divine inspiration exhorts the believers of Corinth to "Come out from among them" (2 Corinthians 6:17). Separation is setting apart or coming apart. It involves the separation, spiritual and moral, from those persons, places, pleasures and pursuits where God is left out.

Chapter 6. The Lord's Supper (Breaking of Bread or Communion)

The Lord Jesus Christ desires that every believer should remember Him in His death as often as possible until He returns. The Christian celebrates with other believers this 'remembrance feast' out of love and obedience to the Lord. Whenever we remember His death we also rejoice in His triumphant resurrection. We know that the Lord Jesus Christ is alive and will return to the air to receive His saints. What a joyous anticipation!

Chapter 7. The Christian and the Word of God

The Bible, which is the word of God with its message of salvation, changes lives, provides a firm foundation for the Christian and society. Jesus, who is the bringer of salvation, is its central theme. The word of God is food for spiritual growth and development. Read the Bible and be well fed. A daily 'quiet time', in addition to memorising key Bible verses is profitable. The word of God is the truth and the only standard by which best judgements must be made.

Chapter 8. Prayer in the Life of the Christian

Prayer is not only speaking to God but listening to Him and coming in line with His will. God, as heavenly Father, does hear and answer the prayers of His children according to His will. The Christian should watch and pray along with learning God's Word in order to overcome temptations. Jesus prayed constantly when He was here on earth. He exhorts us to pray always and not to resort to losing heart. Jesus says that when we come to Him in prayer, we should forgive anyone against whom we have a complaint. This being accomplished, our heavenly Father will forgive us of our trespasses against Him.

Chapter 9. The Old Nature and the New Nature

Yes, the Christian having been born again, becoming a new creation in Christ, is given a new nature (Spiritual or Godly nature) but is still in possession of the old Adamic nature. During this life, the believer experiences constant conflict between the two natures as both the old and the new are opposed to each other. The new nature cannot sin and because God is in control of the believer's life, the new nature will triumph over the old.

Chapter 10. Some Distinguishing Qualities of a Growing Christian

The apostle Peter presents three distinguishing qualities of a growing Christian. A healthy and growing Christian will: (1) love other Christians, (2) lay aside all evil, and (3) long for the pure milk of the Word. It is good to check yourself and to examine yourself as a believer as to whether you are exhibiting true Christian characteristics in your spiritual life and are growing.

Chapter 11. Adjusting Your Christian Life to God

The life of the Christian is one that is set apart for God. You should hear what God says and do what God says. God is all-wise and can be trusted. Trusting and obeying God always pleases Him and brings joy and satisfaction even when intense challenges are encountered.

Chapter 12. Love and the Christian

The best love is agape love, and this love should be displayed by the Christian and be seen by the world around. Jesus taught that when the world sees Christians displaying love among themselves the world will be convinced that the Christians are His followers. As Christians, our love is firstly to God and then to others.

Chapter 13. Forgiveness and the Christian

From a Biblical perspective, forgiveness is the cancelling by God of the sinner's debt and guilt on the basis of Christ's death for sinners. The conditions are repentance and faith in Jesus Christ ("In Him, we have redemption through His blood, the forgiveness of sins, according to the riches of His grace" – Ephesians 1:7). If it seems I cannot forgive or I am determined never to forgive, I must remember how much I have been forgiven.

Chapter 14. Temptation and the Christian

For the Christian, temptation is a fact of life as long as he lives on the earth. Our Lord Jesus Christ experienced temptations and overcame them. Christians are encouraged to follow Christ's example and resist temptation. The word of God, the prayer of faith and the help of the Holy Spirit will gain us victory. Thanks be to God! Every Christian can experience the joy and peace of spiritual happiness and satisfaction by being victorious over temptation and sin.

Chapter 15. Joy and the Christian

The Christian has a deep-seated heart and soul joy based on the contentment and satisfaction in God Himself. It is a gift from God and should be evidenced in the Christian here on earth even during challenging times. Joy is one of the segments of the fruit of the indwelling Holy Spirit. Christians have a rock-solid assurance that it is impossible for anyone to take away their place in heaven. Knowing that the Christian is heaven-bound and not hell-bound gives great joy peace and satisfaction to the heart.